FOR ORGANS, PIANOS & ELECTRONIC KEYBOARDS

E-Z PLAY TODAY

56

JERSEY BOYS

The story of Frankie Valli & The Four Seasons

2	BIG GIRLS DON'T CRY
5	BIG MAN IN TOWN
8	BYE BYE BABY (BABY GOODBYE)
14	CAN'T TAKE MY EYES OFF OF YOU
18	DECEMBER 1963 (OH, WHAT A NIGHT)
22	FALLEN ANGEL
11	LET'S HANG ON
26	MY BOYFRIEND'S BACK
32	MY EYES ADORED YOU
29	RAG DOLL
38	SHERRY
44	STAY
41	WALK LIKE A MAN
46	WHO LOVES YOU
50	WORKING MY WAY BACK TO YOU
53	Registration Guide

ISBN 978-1-4950-0077-5

HAL•LEONARD®
CORPORATION
7777 W. BLUEMOUND RD. P.O. BOX 13819 MILWAUKEE, WI 53213

Visit Hal Leonard Online at
www.halleonard.com

Big Girls Don't Cry

Registration 9
Rhythm: Rock or Pops

Words and Music by Bob Crewe
and Bob Gaudio

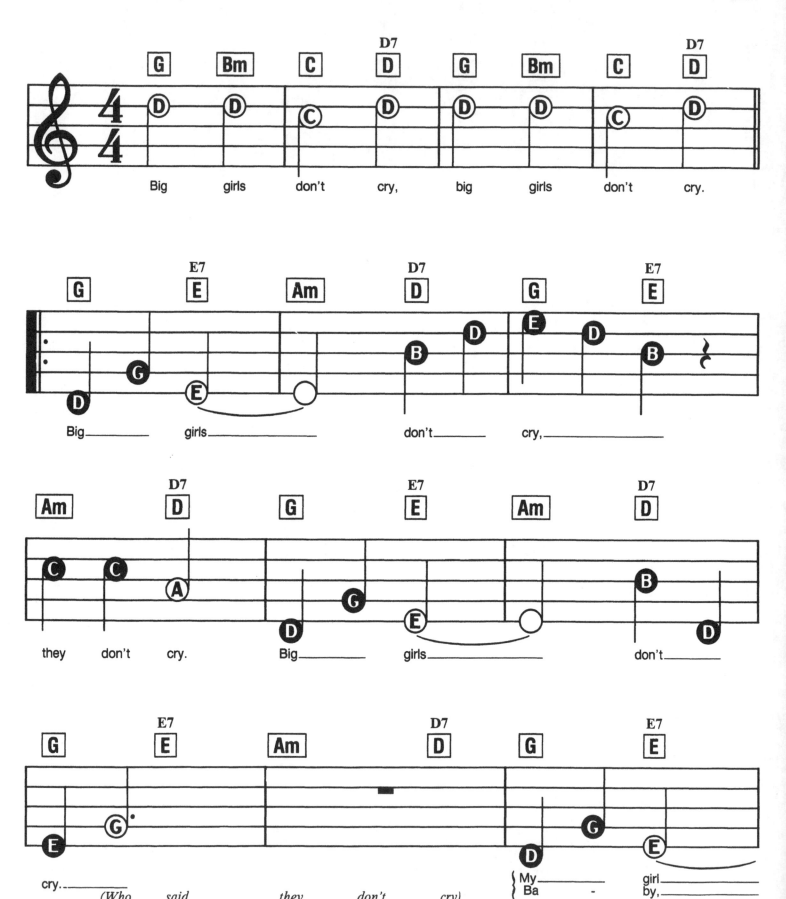

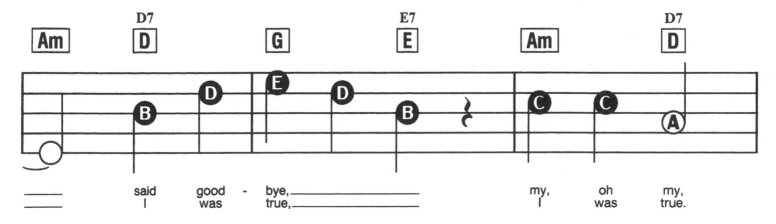

said good - bye,_____ my, oh my,
I was true,_____ I was true.

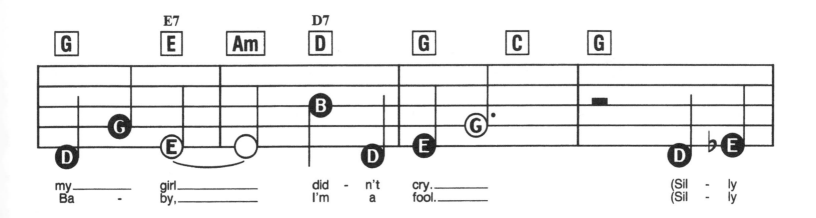

my_____ girl_____ did - n't cry._____ (Sil - ly
Ba - by,_____ I'm a fool._____ (Sil - ly

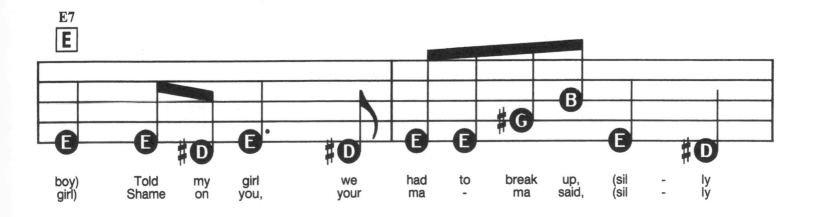

boy) Told my girl we had to break up, (sil - ly
girl) Shame on you, your ma - ma said, (sil - ly

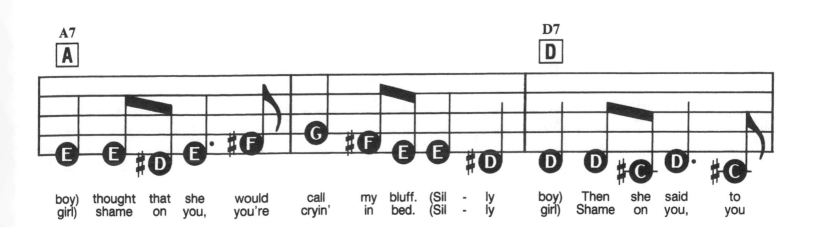

boy) thought that she would call my bluff. (Sil - ly
girl) shame on you, you're cryin' in bed. (Sil - ly

boy) Then she said to
girl) Shame on you, to you

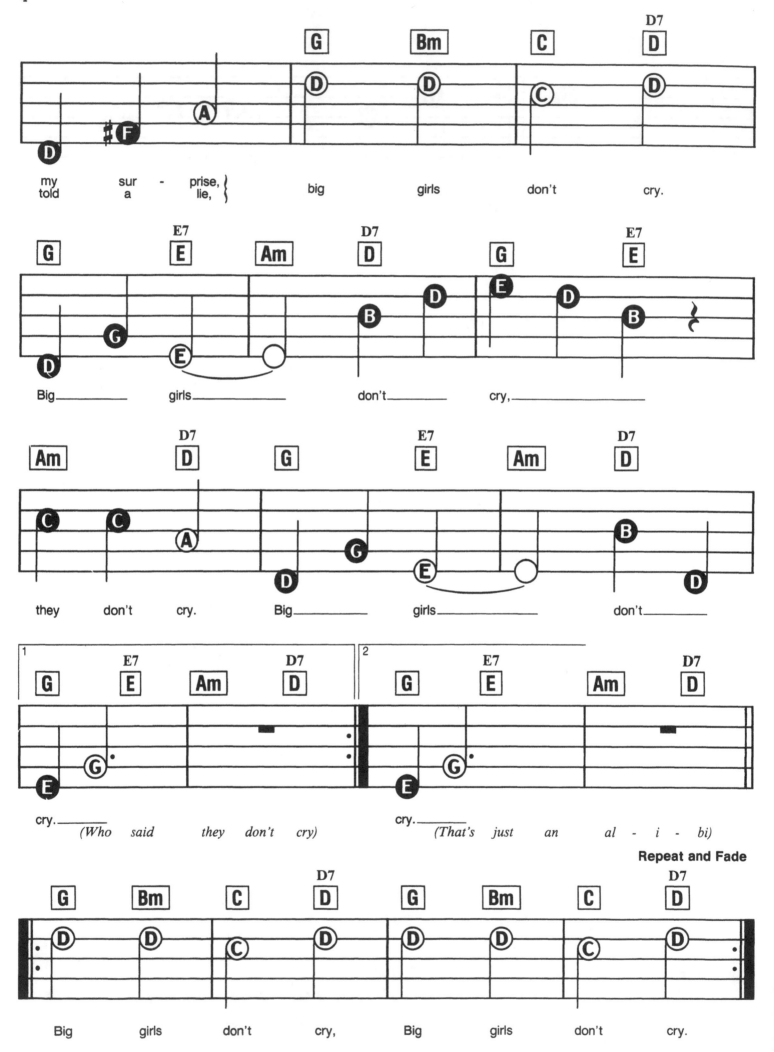

Big Man in Town

Registration 4
Rhythm: Rock

Words and Music by
Bob Gaudio

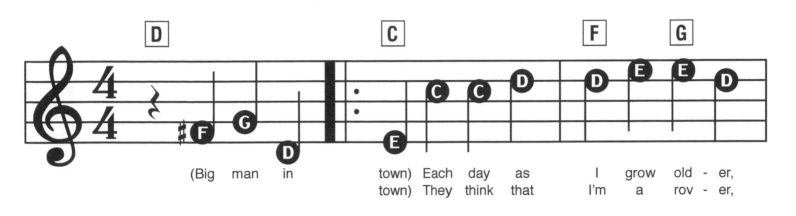

(Big man in town) Each day as I grow old - er,
town) They think as that I'm a rov - er,

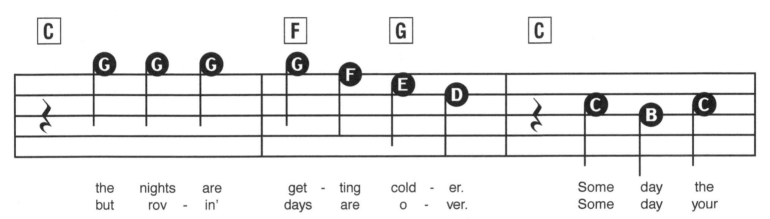

the nights are get - ting cold - er.
but rov - in' days are o - ver.

Some day the
Some day your

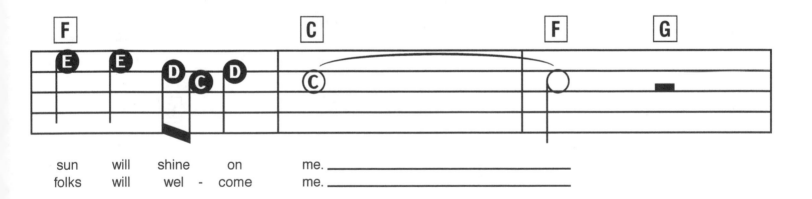

sun will shine on me. _____
folks will wel - come me. _____

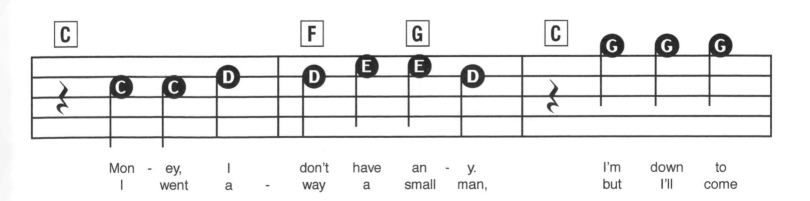

Mon - ey, I don't have an - y.
I went a - way a small man,

I'm down to
but I'll come

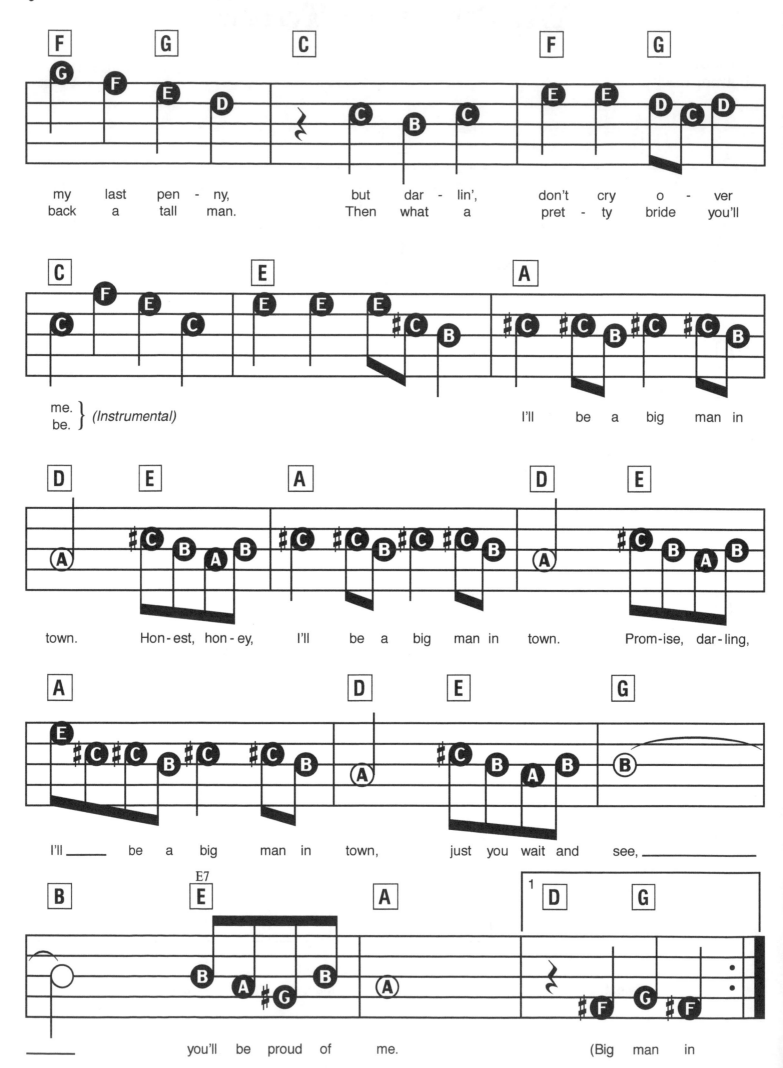

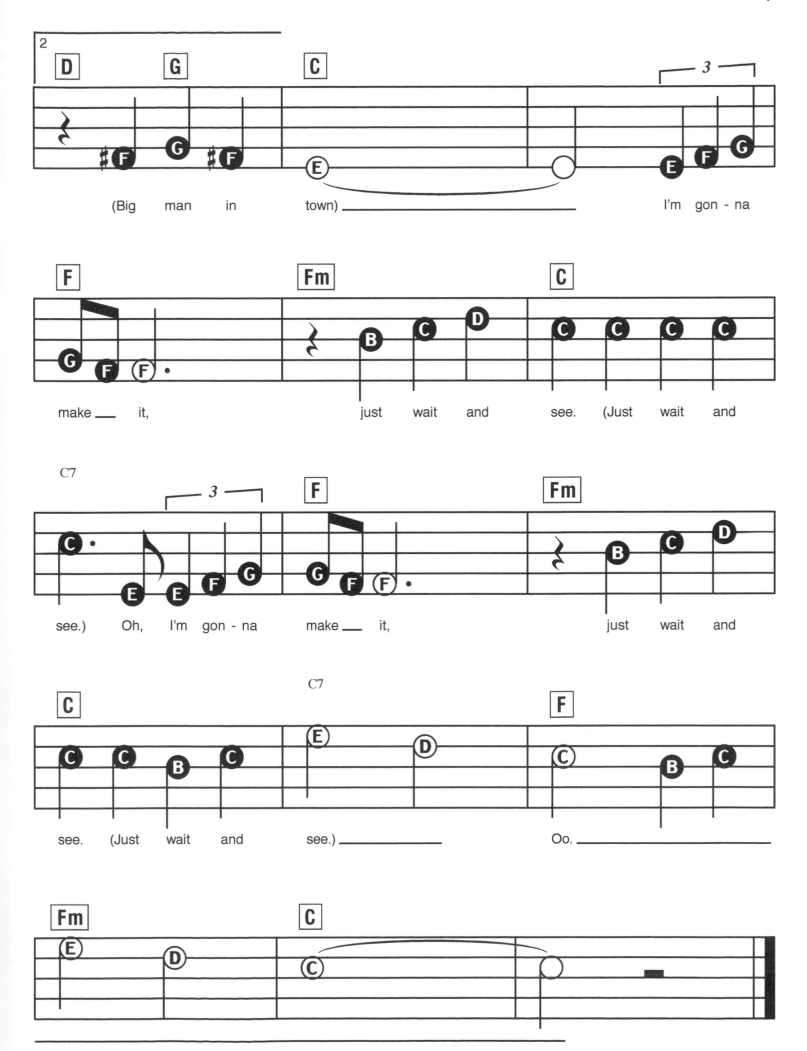

Bye Bye Baby
(Baby Goodbye)

Registration 2
Rhythm: Swing or Rock

Words and Music by Bob Crewe
and Bob Gaudio

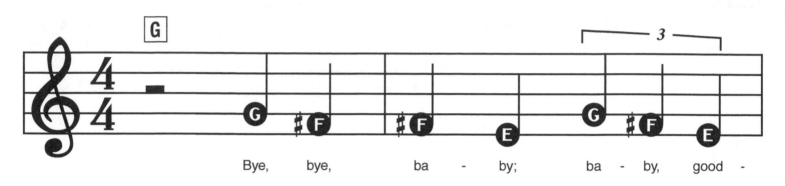

Bye, bye, ba - by; ba - by, good -

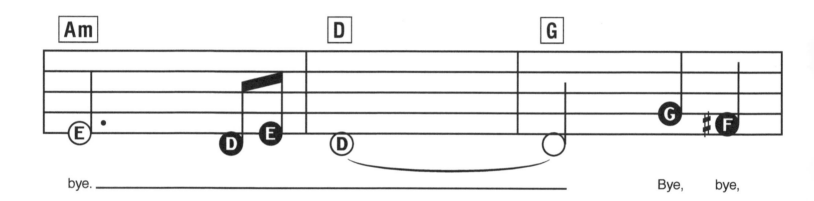

bye. ___ Bye, bye,

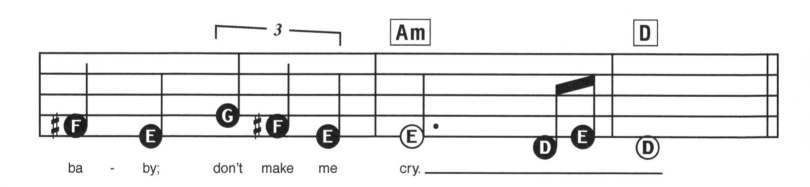

ba - by; don't make me cry. ___

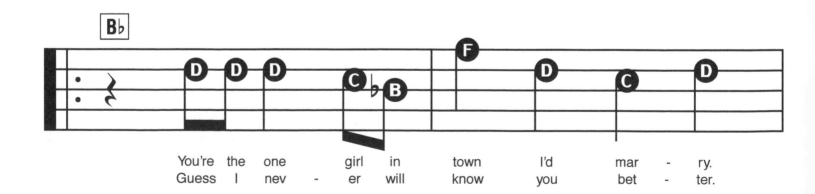

You're the one girl in town I'd mar - ry.
Guess I nev - er will know you bet - ter.

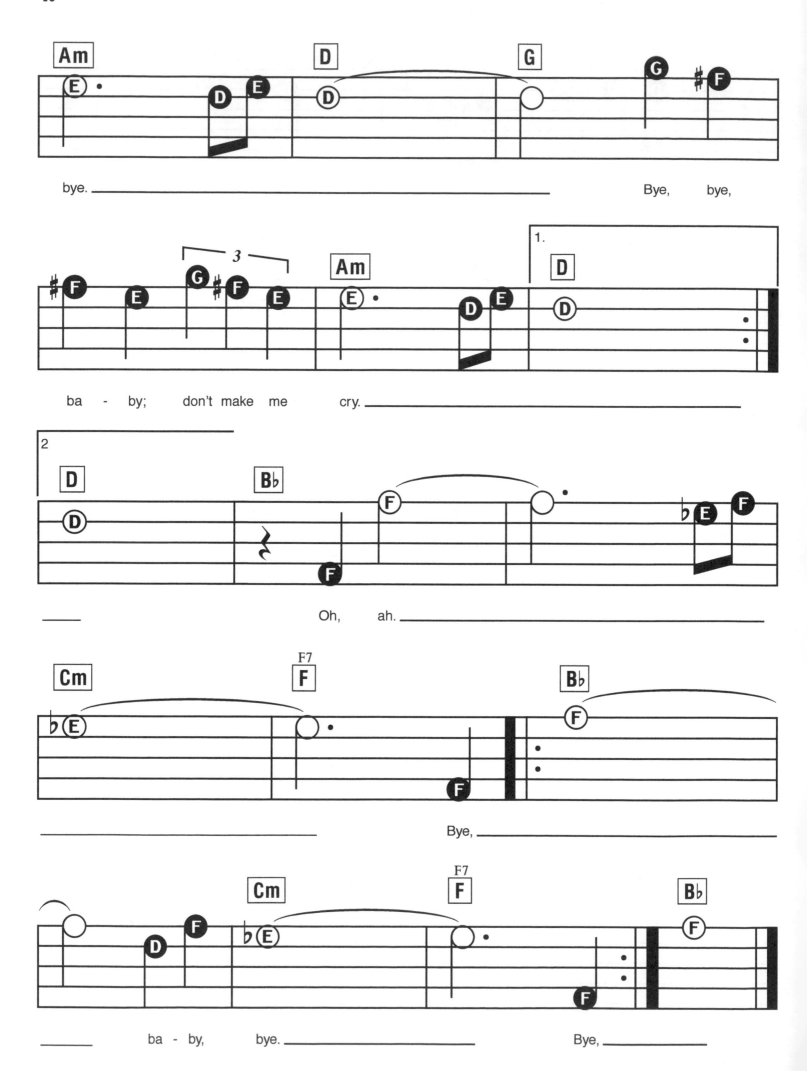

Let's Hang On

Registration 4
Rhythm: Rock or 8-Beat

Words and Music by Bob Crewe,
Denny Randell and Sandy Linzer

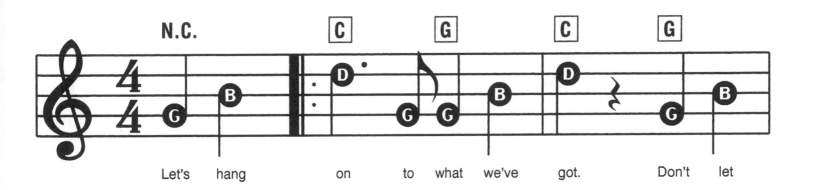

Let's hang on to what we've got. Don't let

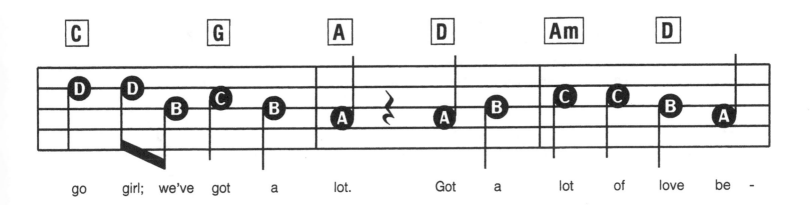

go girl; we've got a lot. Got a lot of love be -

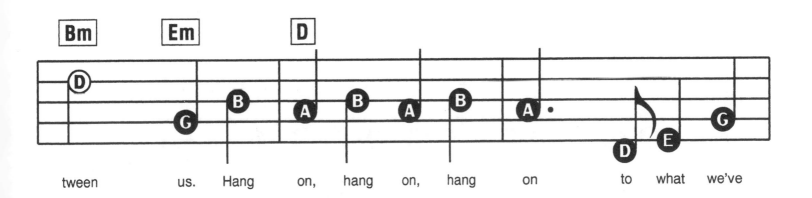

tween us. Hang on, hang on, hang on to what we've

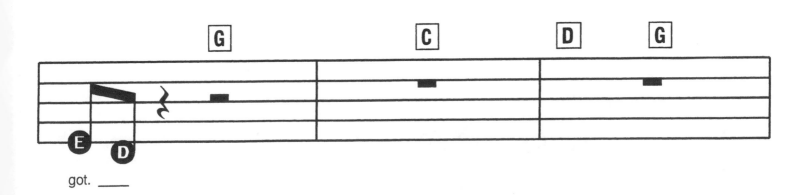

got. ____

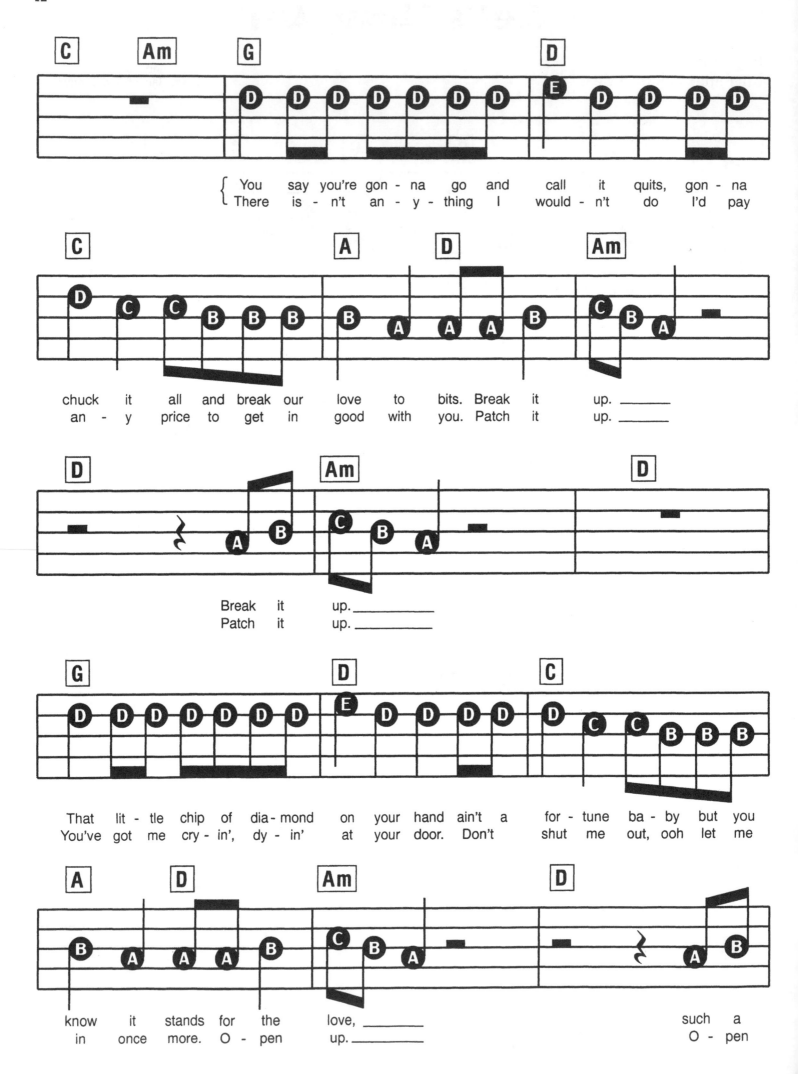

Can't Take My Eyes Off of You

Registration 4
Rhythm: Medium Rock

Words and Music by Bob Crewe
and Bob Gaudio

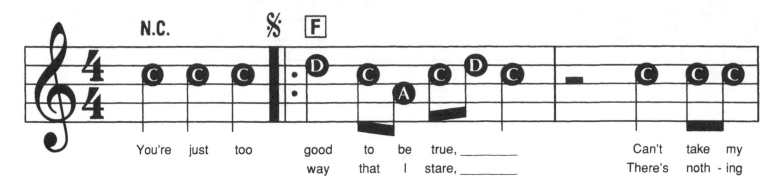

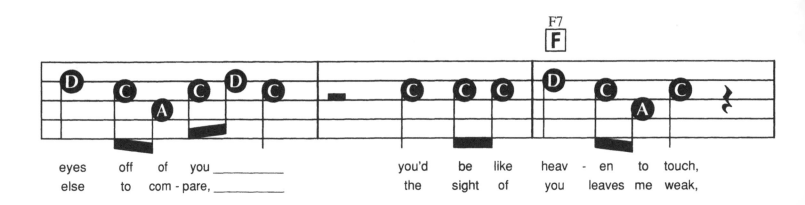

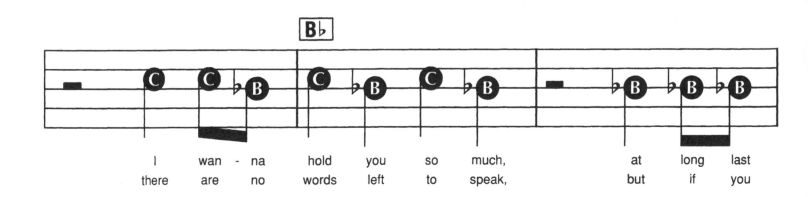

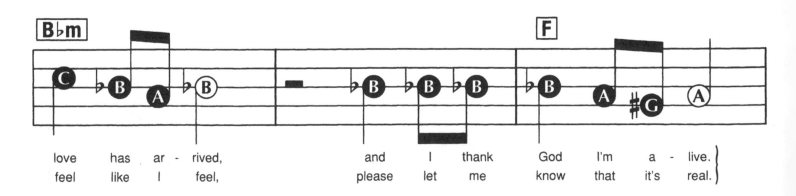

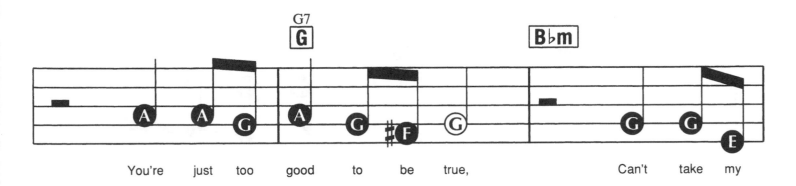

You're just too good to be true,   Can't take my

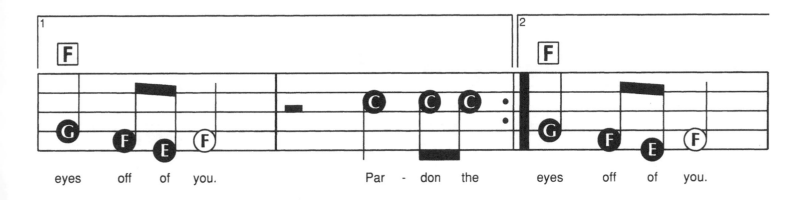

eyes off of you.   Par - don the   eyes off of you.

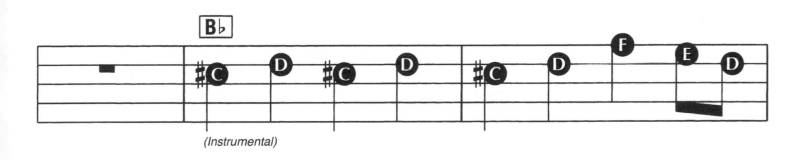

(Instrumental)

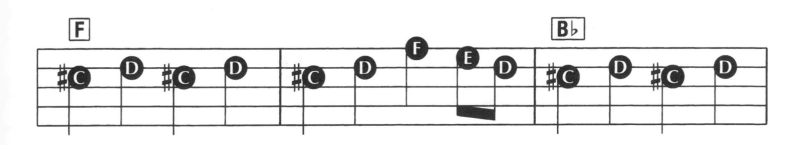

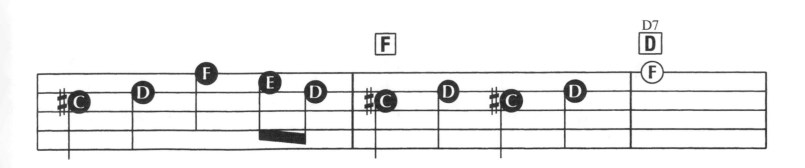

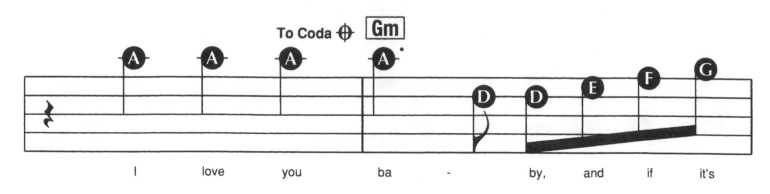

I love you ba - by, and if it's

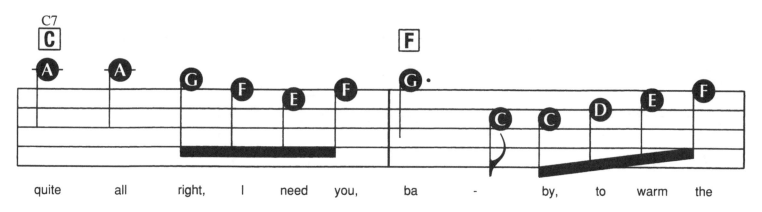

quite all right, I need you, ba - by, to warm the

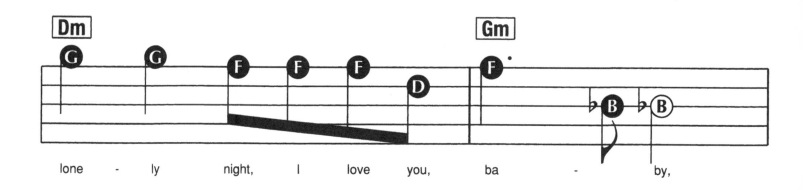

lone - ly night, I love you, ba - by,

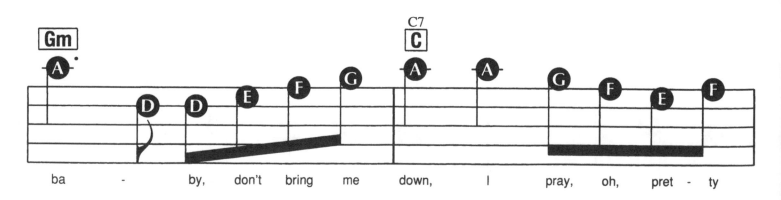

trust in me when I _____ say: Oh, pret - ty

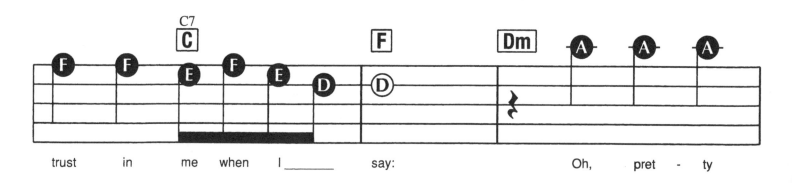

ba - by, don't bring me down, I pray, oh, pret - ty

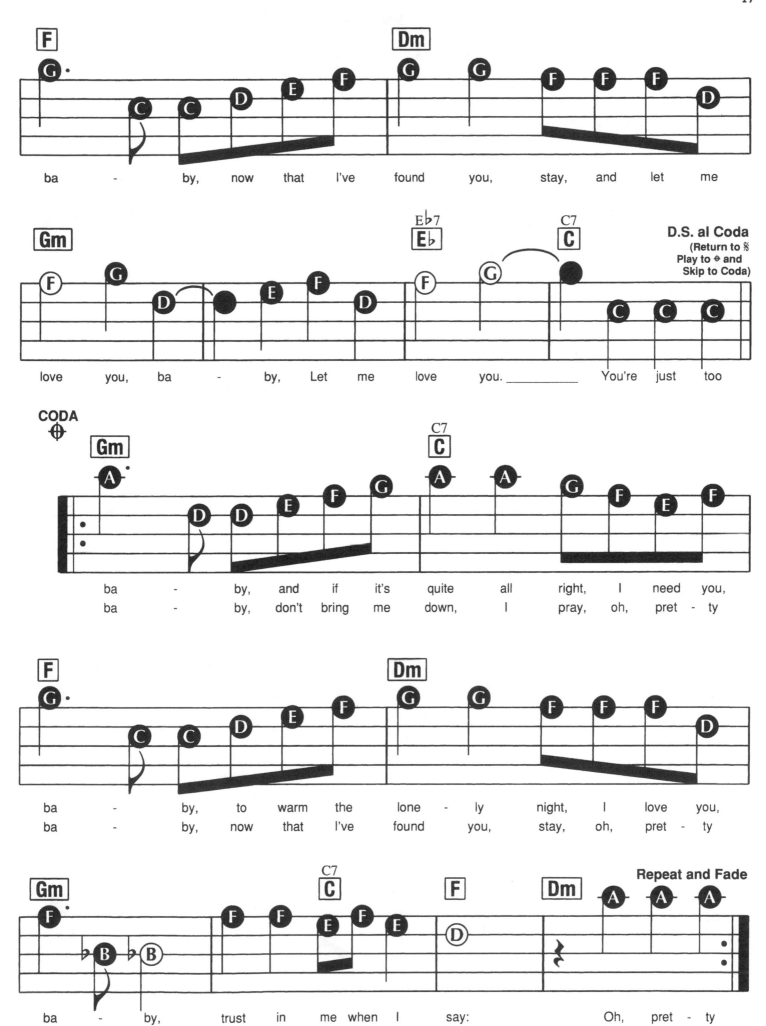

December 1963
(Oh, What a Night)

Registration 7
Rhythm: 8-Beat or Rock

Words and Music by Robert Gaudio
and Judy Parker

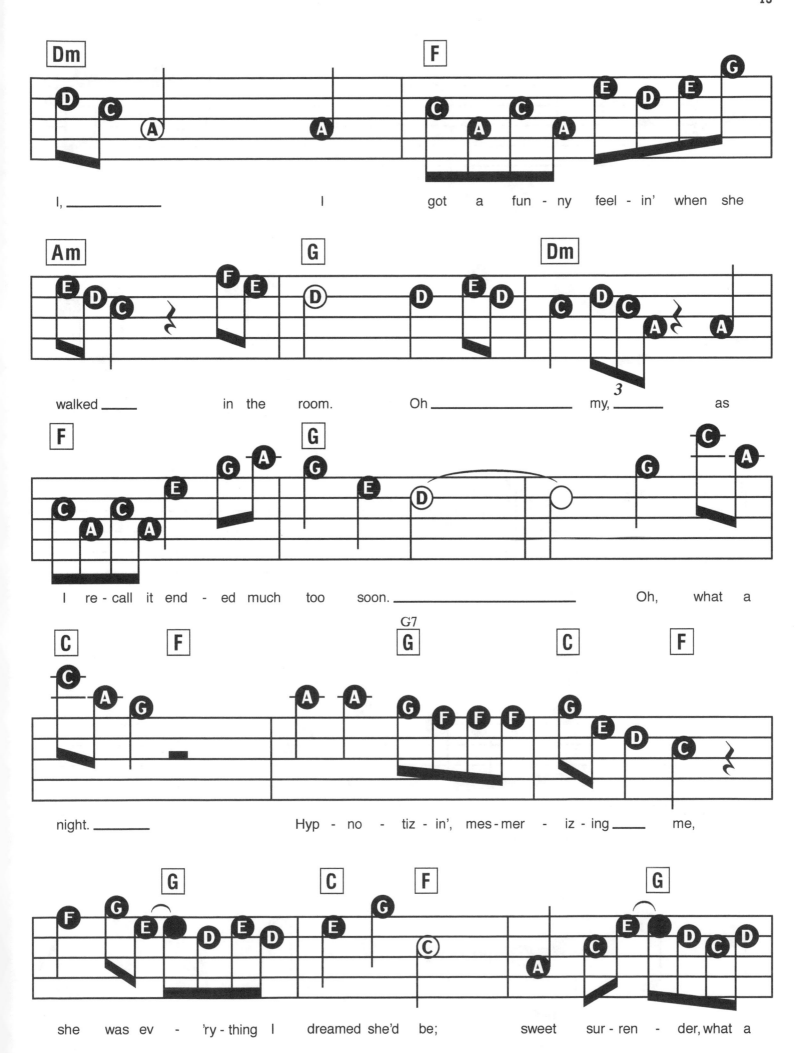

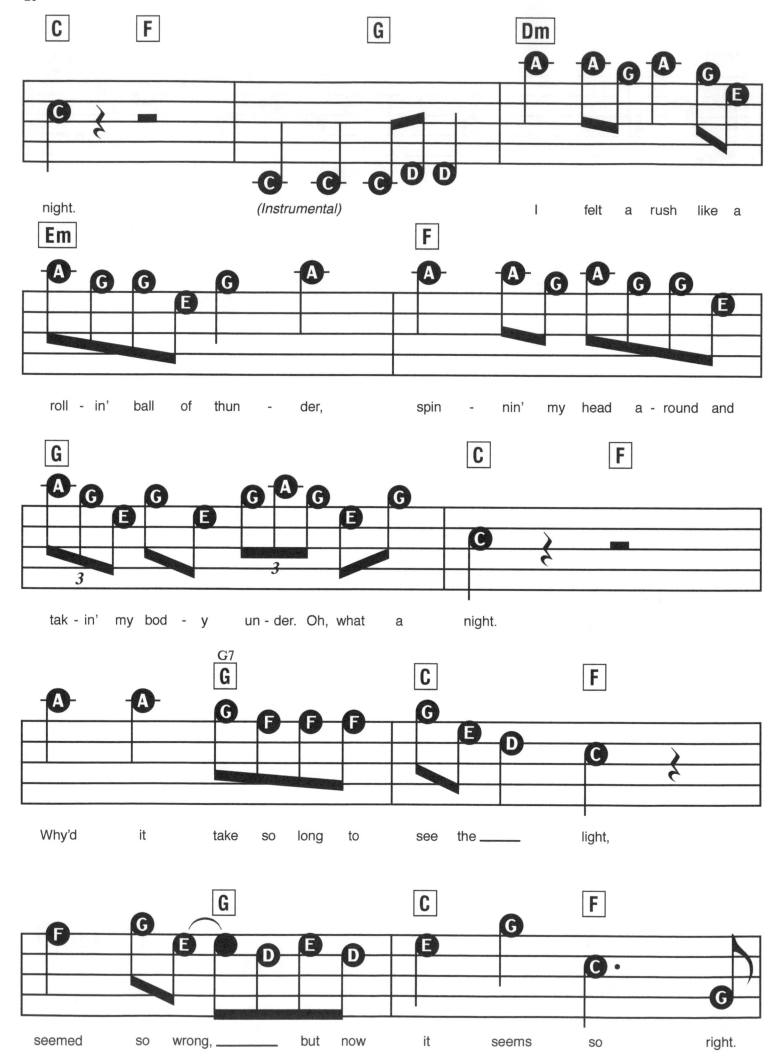

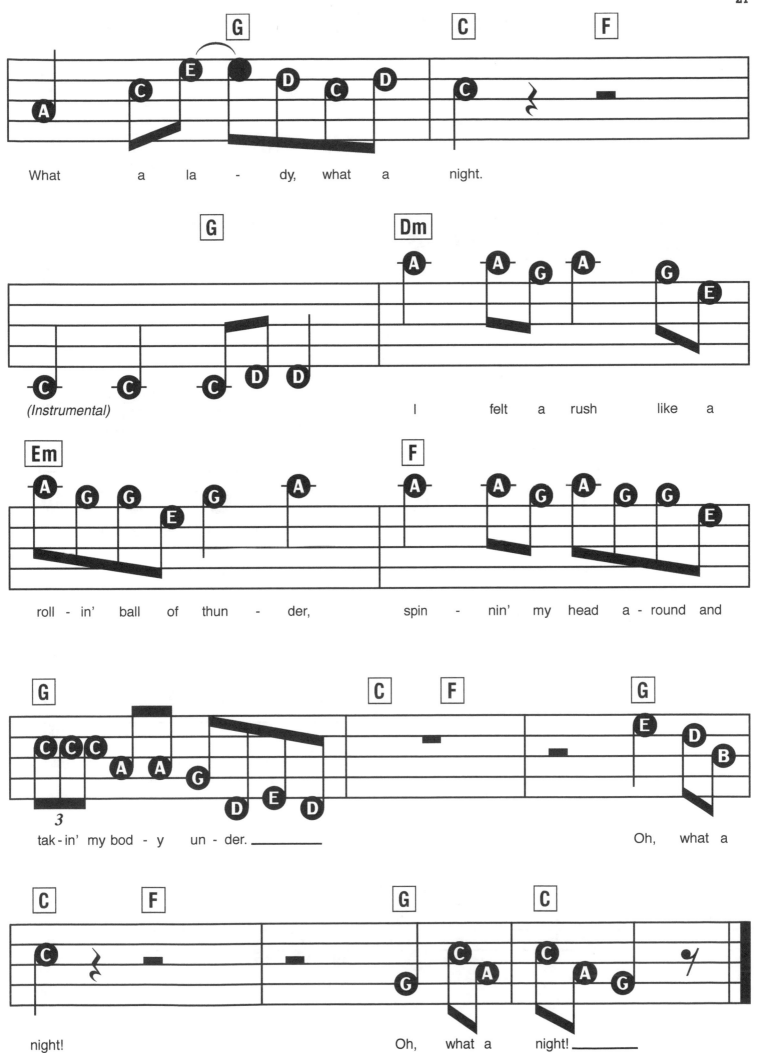

Fallen Angel

Registration 4
Rhythm: Ballad

Words and Music by Guy Fletcher
and Doug Flett

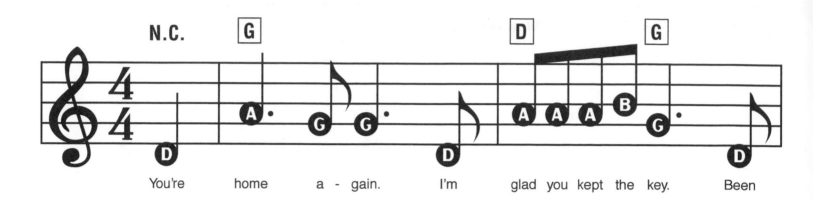

You're home a - gain. I'm glad you kept the key. Been

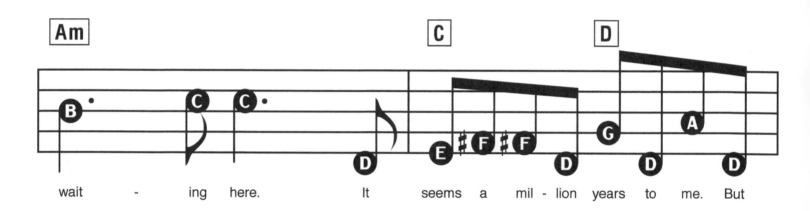

wait - ing here. It seems a mil - lion years to me. But

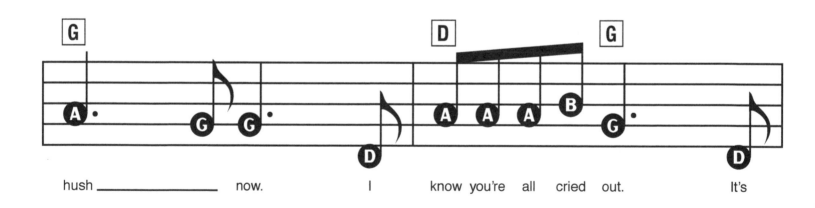

hush _____ now. I know you're all cried out. It's

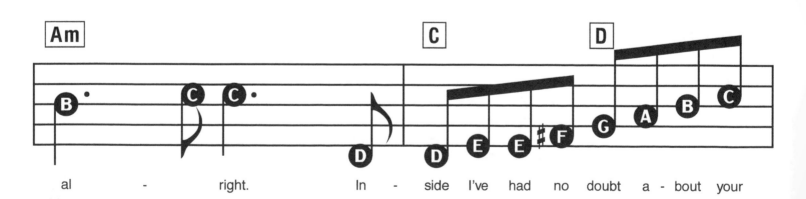

al - right. In - side I've had no doubt a - bout your

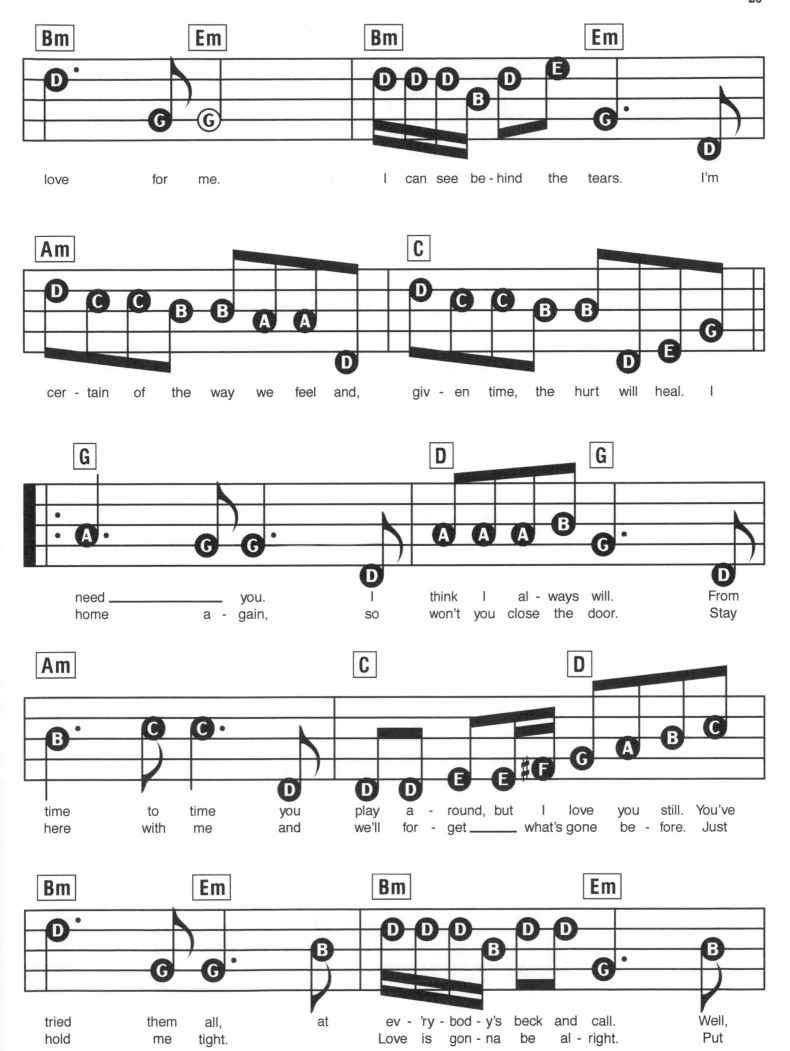

24

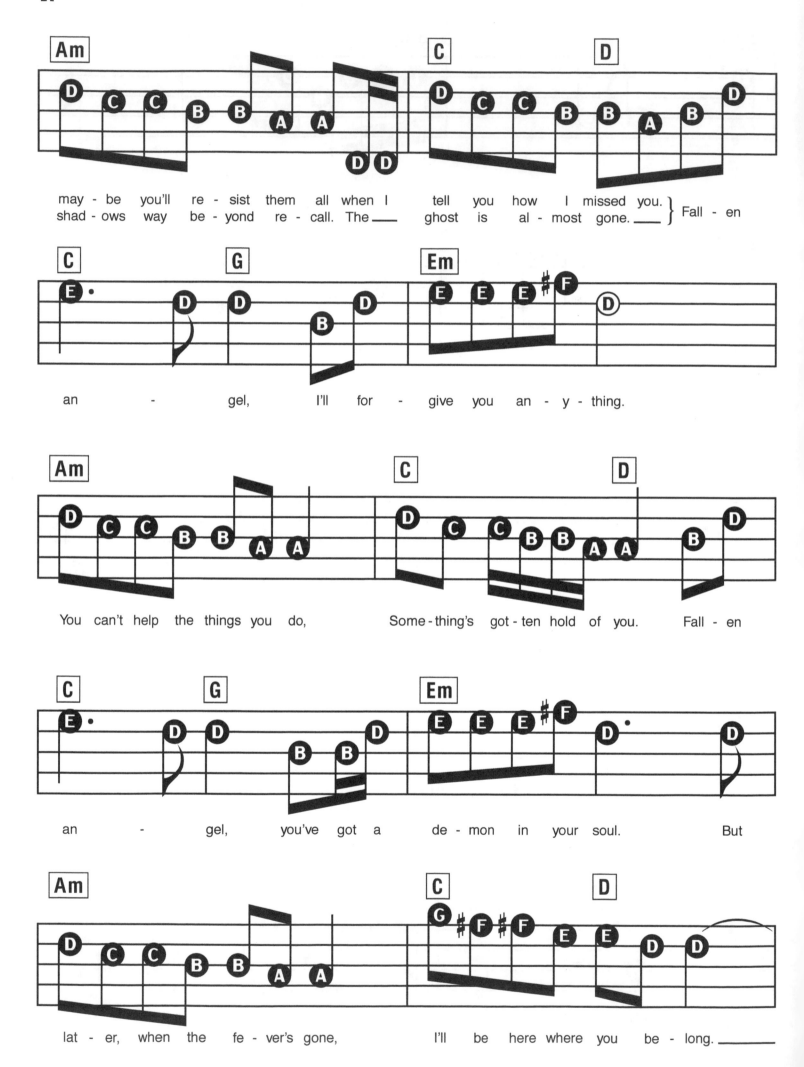

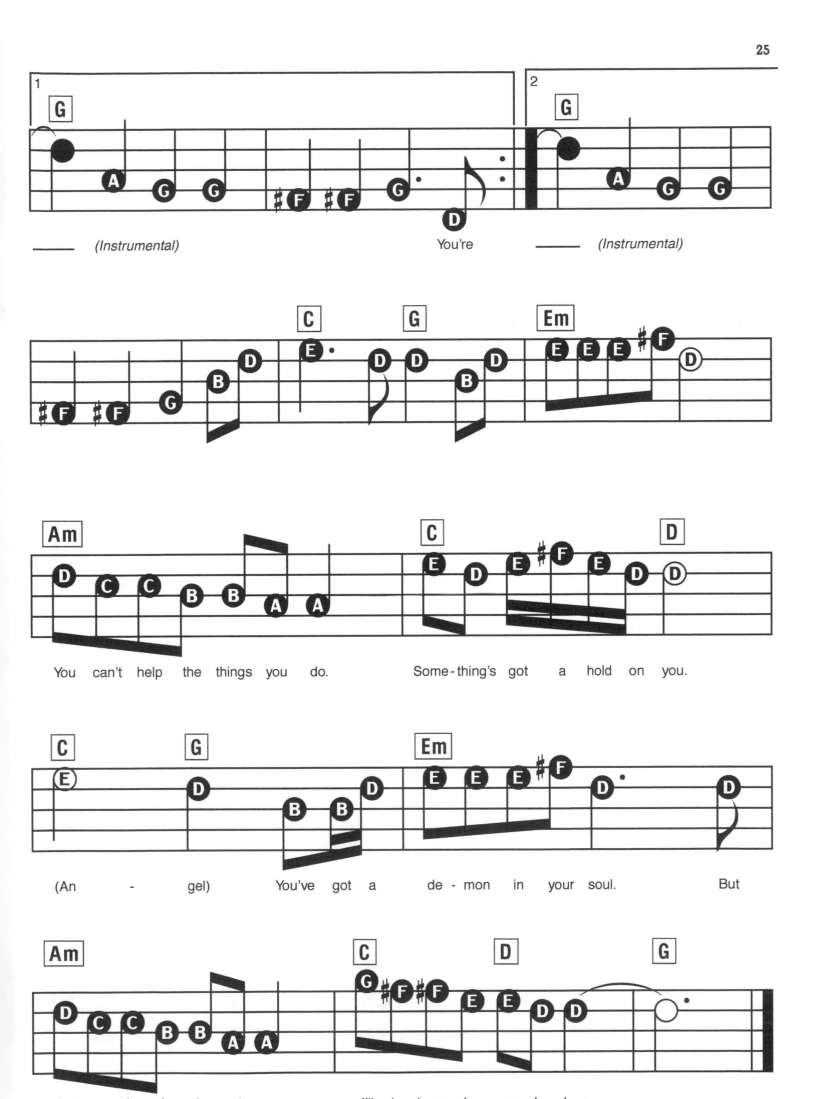

My Boyfriend's Back

Registration 2
Rhythm: Rock

Words and Music by Robert Feldman,
Gerald Goldstein and Richard Gottehrer

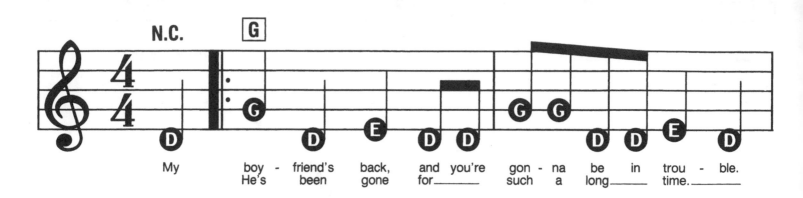

My boy - friend's back, and you're gon - na be in trou - ble.
He's been gone for such a long time.

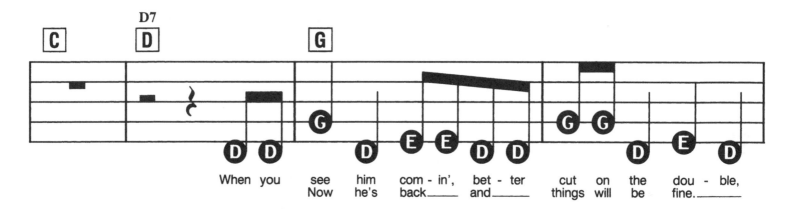

When you see him com - in', bet - ter cut on the dou - ble,
Now he's back and things will be fine.

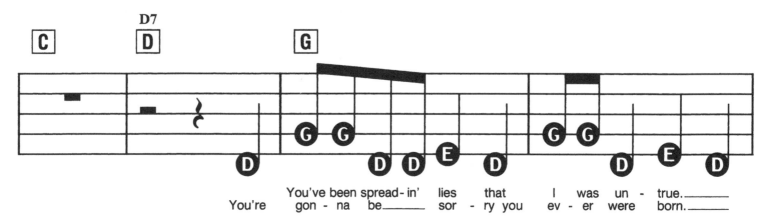

You've been spread - in' lies that I was un - true.
You're gon - na be sor - ry you ev - er were born.

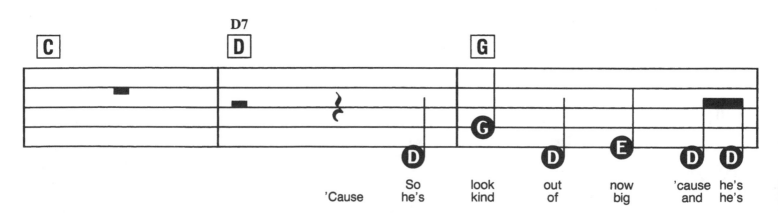

'Cause So he's look kind out of now big 'cause and he's

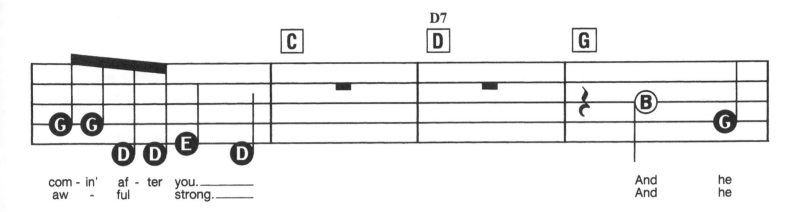

com - in' af - ter you._____ And he
aw - ful strong._____ And he

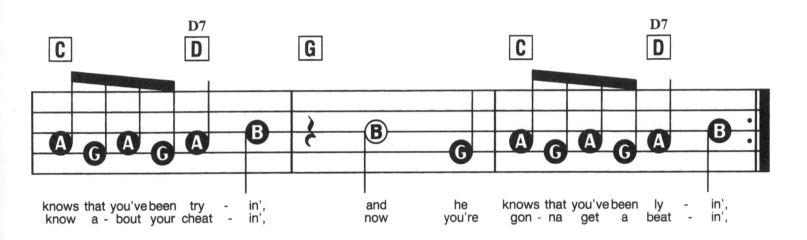

knows that you've been try - in', and he knows that you've been ly - in',
know a - bout your cheat - in', now you're gon - na get a beat - in',

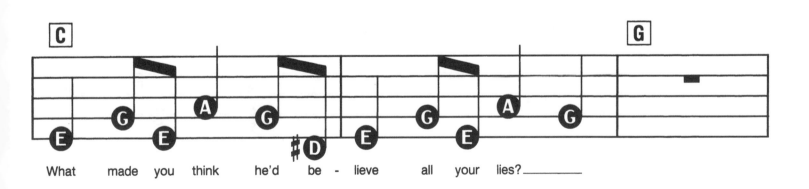

What made you think he'd be - lieve all your lies?_____

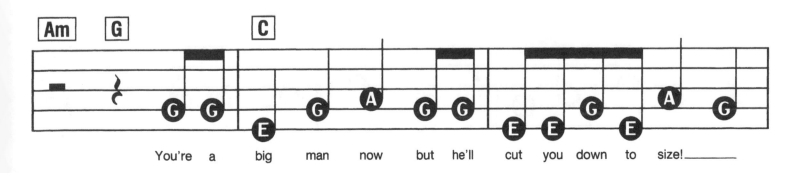

You're a big man now but he'll cut you down to size!_____

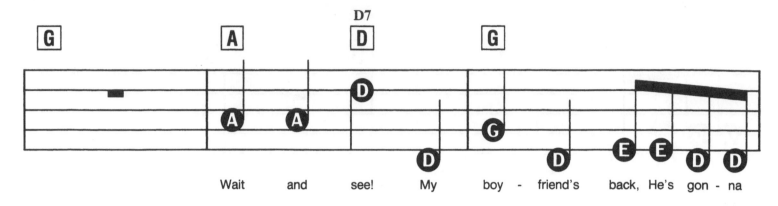

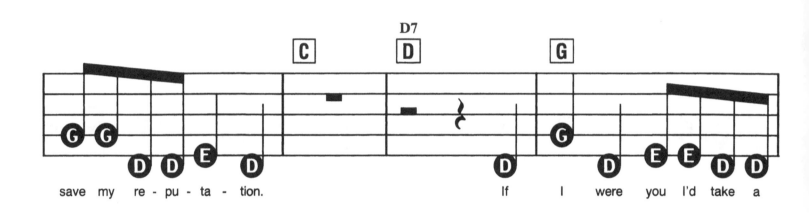

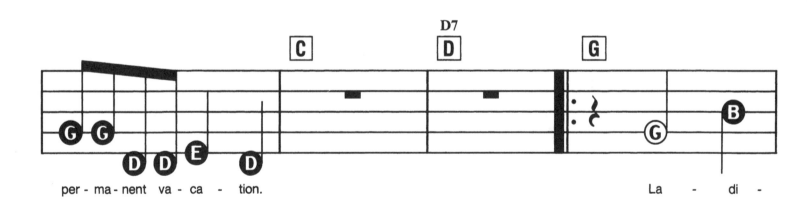

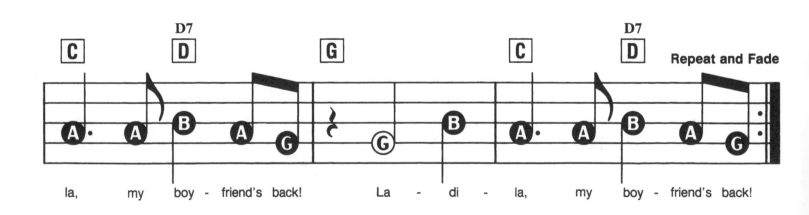

Rag Doll

Registration 1
Rhythm: Rock

Words and Music by Robert Crewe
and Bob Gaudio

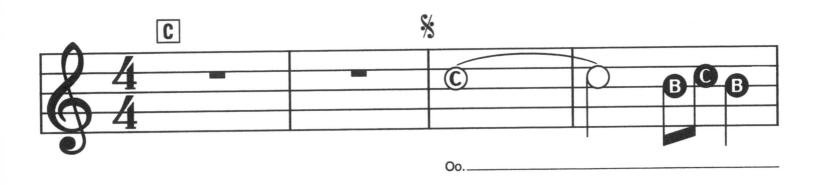

Oo.

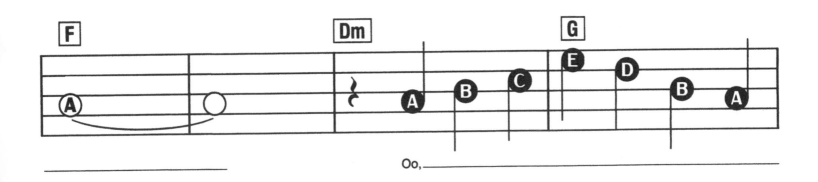

Oo,

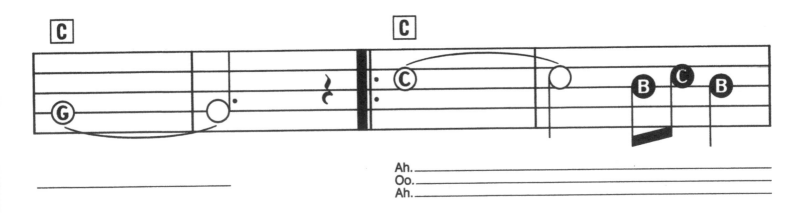

Ah.
Oo.
Ah.

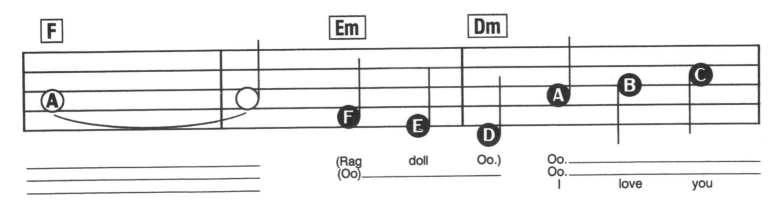

(Rag   doll   Oo.)   Oo.
(Oo)   Oo.
I   love   you

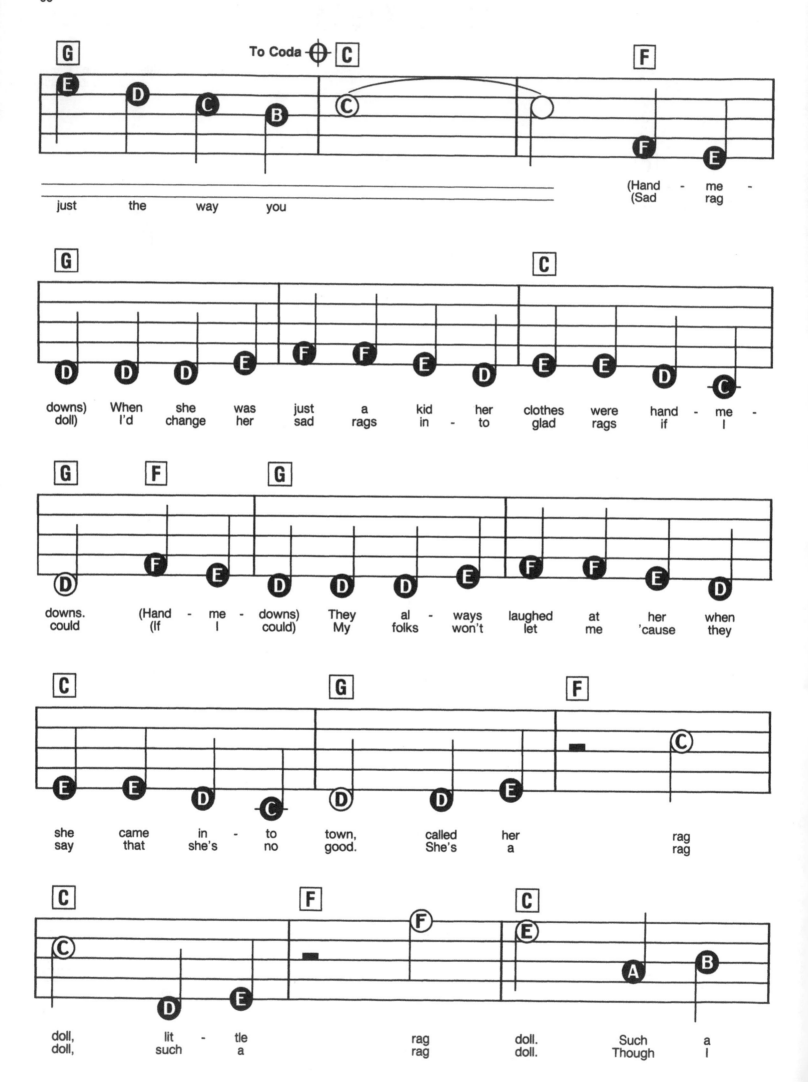

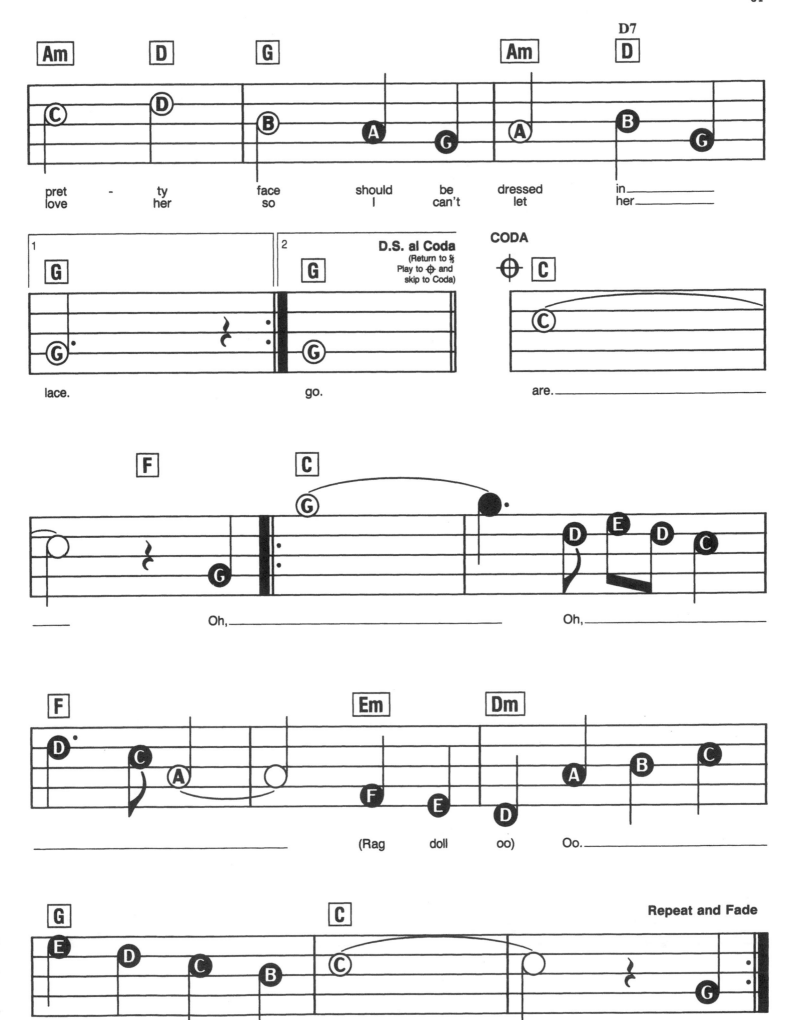

My Eyes Adored You

Registration 4
Rhythm: 8-Beat or Rock

Words and Music by Bob Crewe
and Kenny Nolan

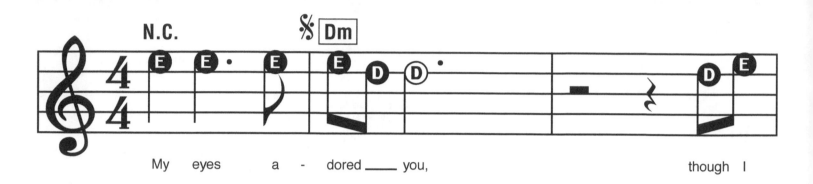

My eyes a - dored ____ you, though I

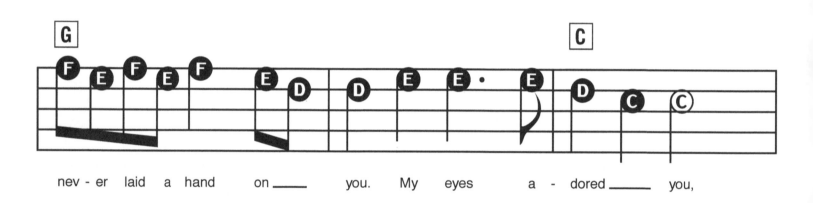

nev - er laid a hand on ____ you. My eyes a - dored ____ you,

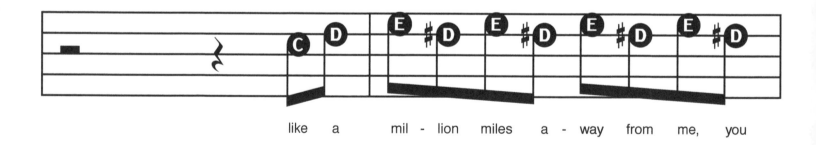

like a mil - lion miles a - way from me, you

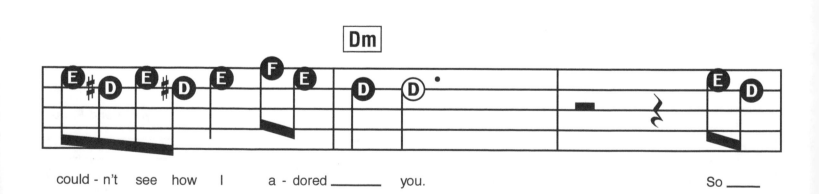

could - n't see how I a - dored ____ you. So ____

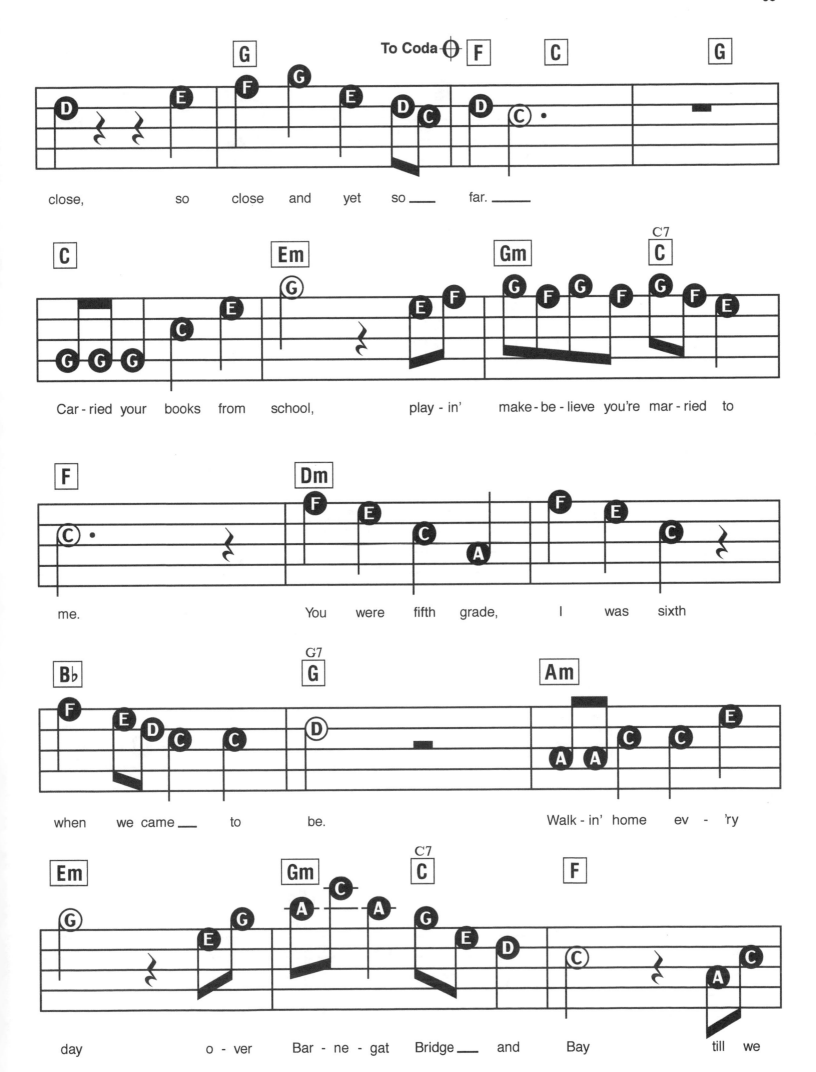

close, so close and yet so ___ far. ___

Car - ried your books from school, play - in' make - be - lieve you're mar - ried to

me. You were fifth grade, I was sixth

when we came ___ to be. Walk - in' home ev - 'ry

day o - ver Bar - ne - gat Bridge ___ and Bay till we

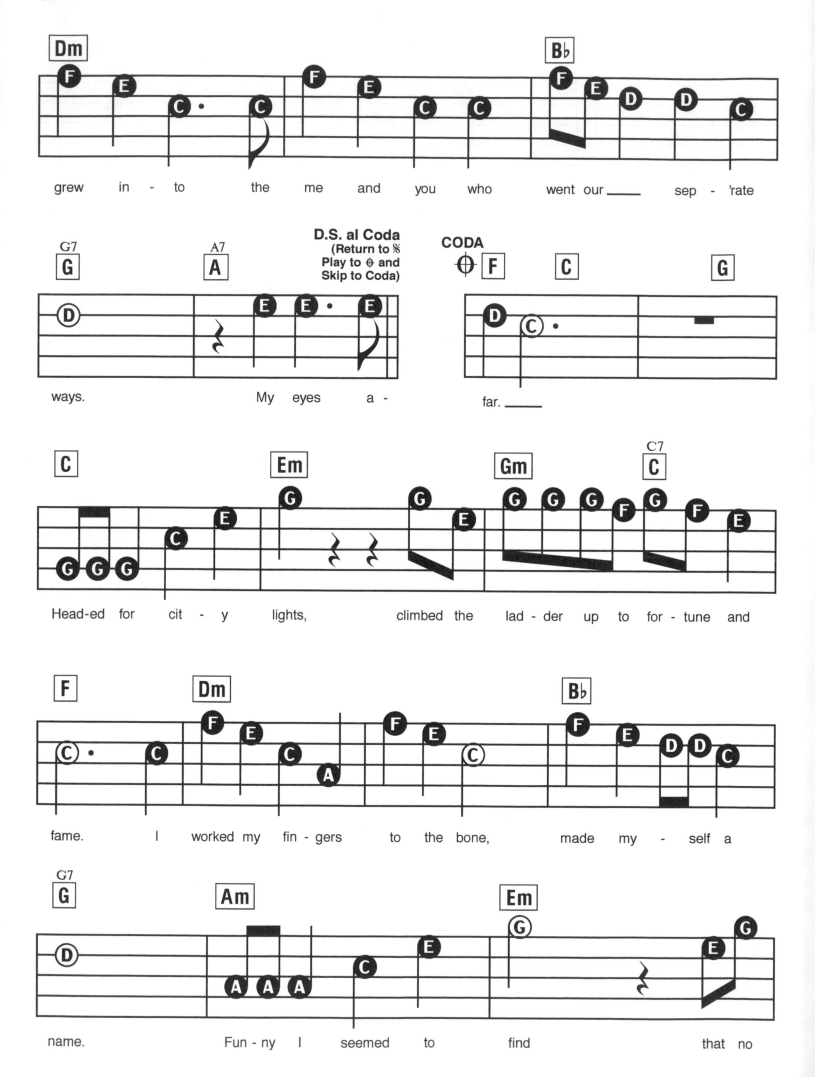

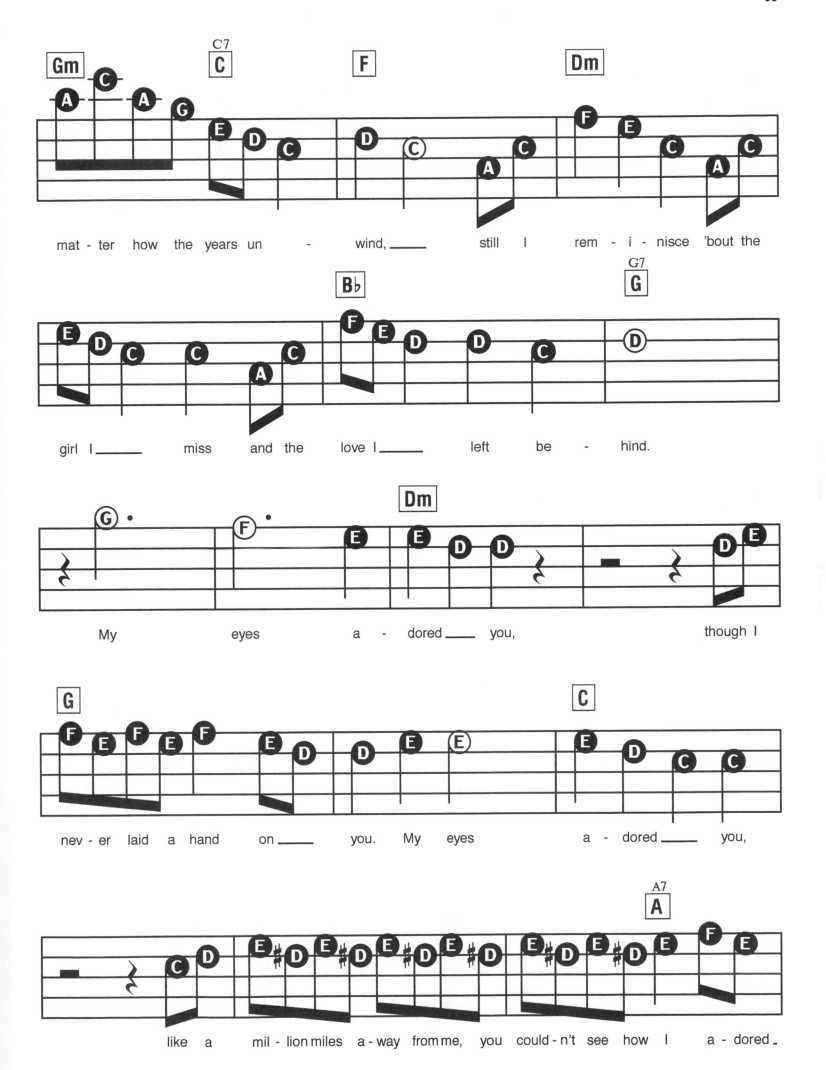

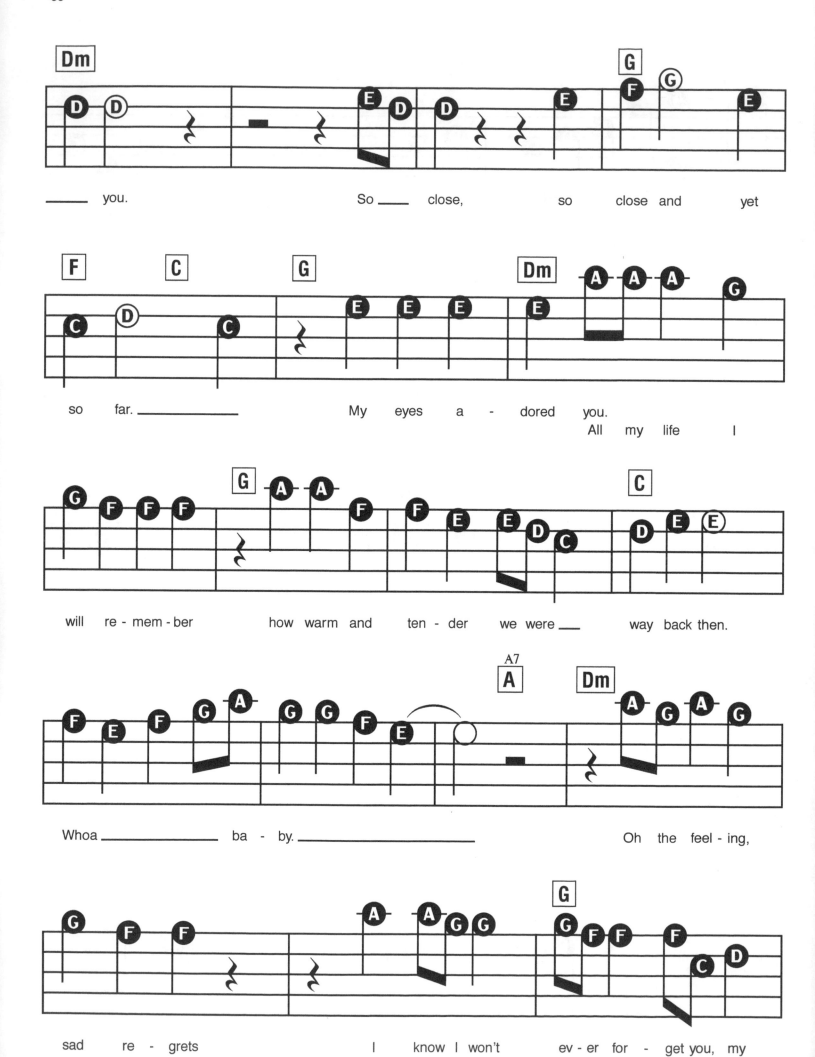

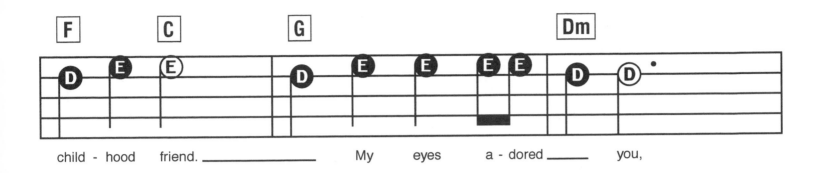

child - hood friend. _____ My eyes a - dored _____ you,

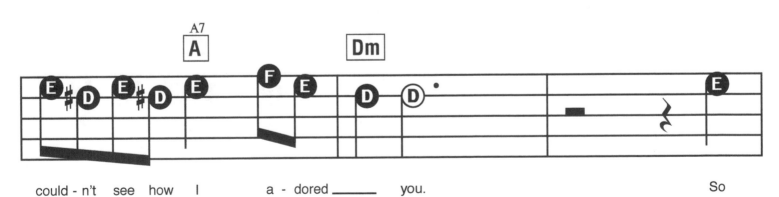

though I nev - er laid a hand on you. My eyes a -

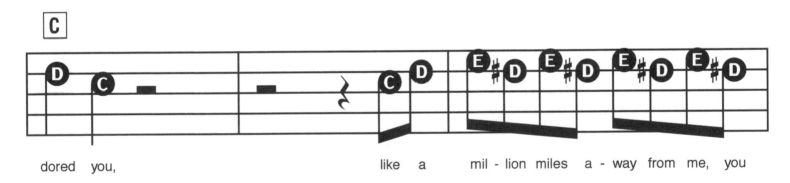

dored you, like a mil - lion miles a - way from me, you

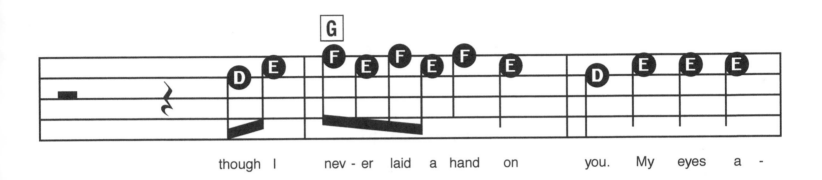

could - n't see how I a - dored _____ you. So

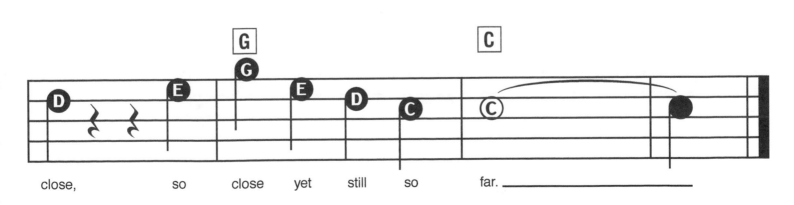

close, so close yet still so far. _____

Sherry

Registration 4
Rhythm: Rock or 8-Beat

Words and Music by
Bob Gaudio

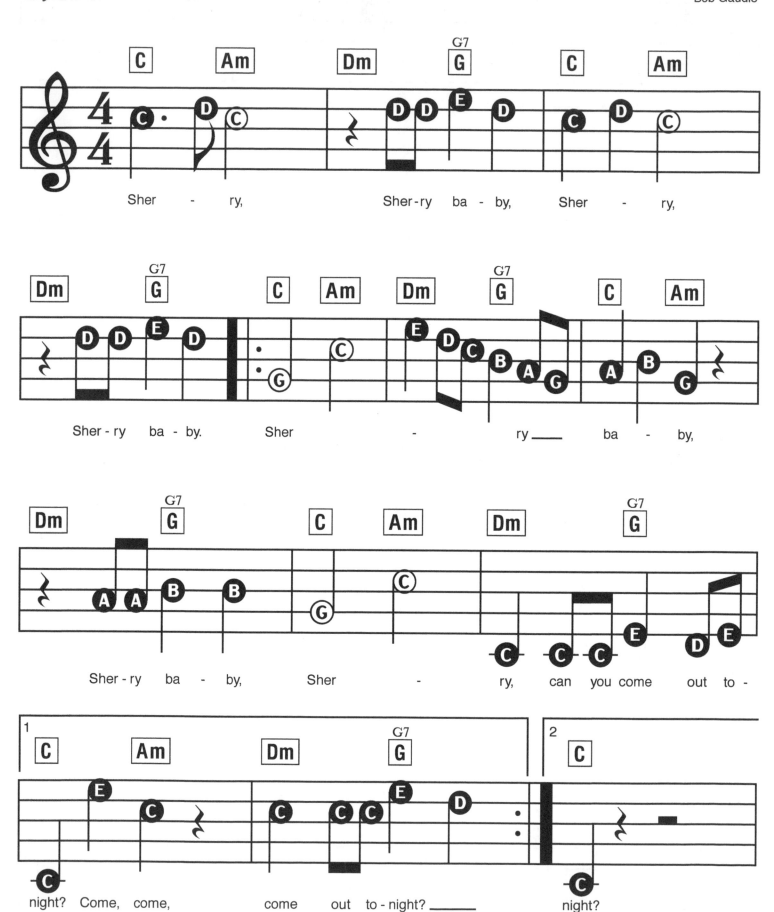

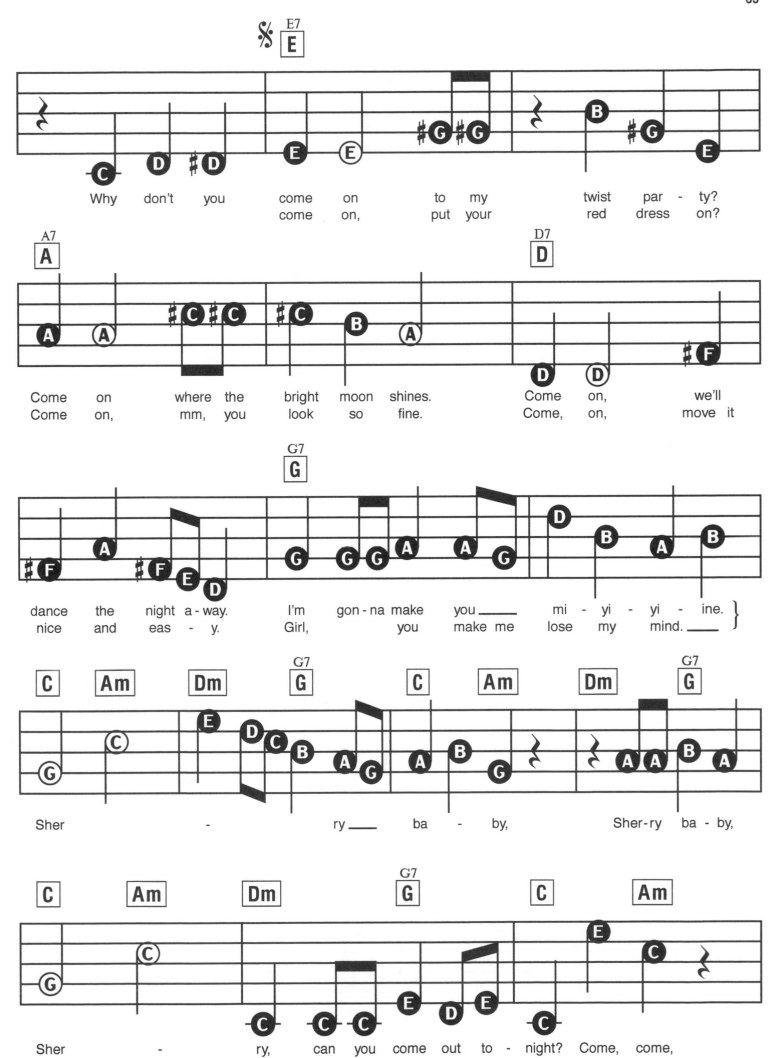

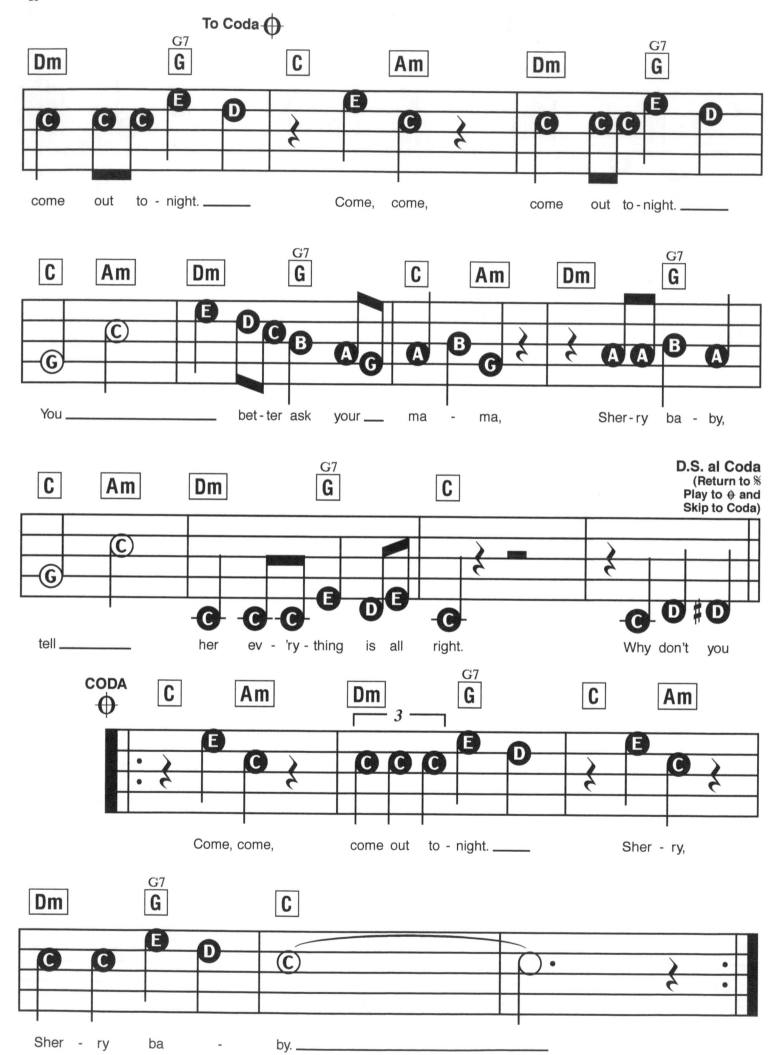

Walk Like a Man

Registration 7
Rhythm: Rock, Fox Trot, or March

Words and Music by Bob Crewe
and Bob Gaudio

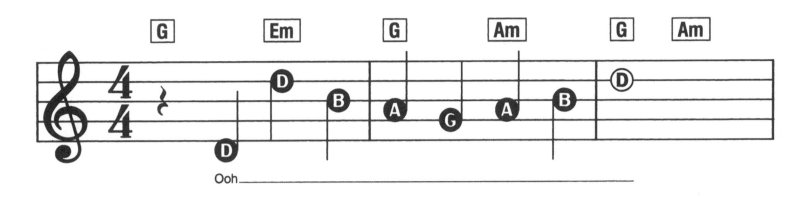

Ooh_____

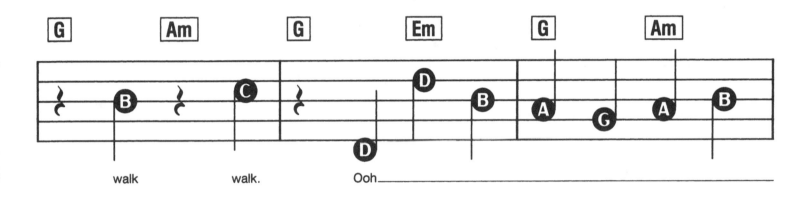

walk   walk.   Ooh_____

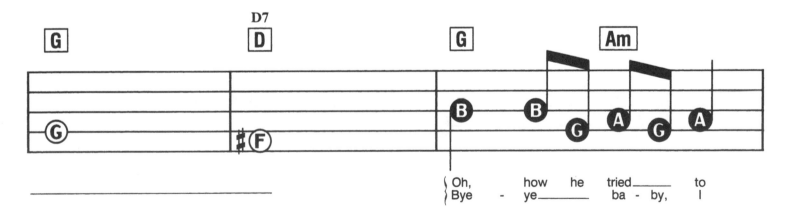

Oh,   how he   tried_____ to
Bye - ye_____ ba - by,   I

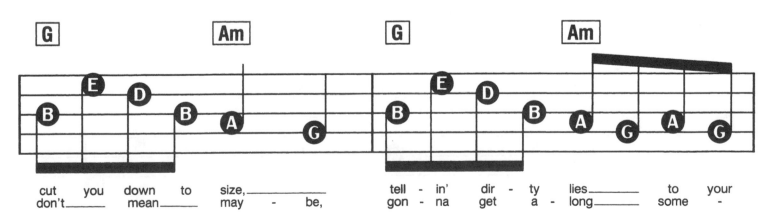

cut   you   down   to   size,_____   to   your
don't_____   mean_____   may - be,   gon - na   get a - long_____   some -

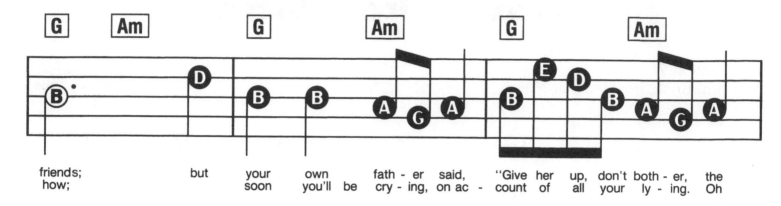

friends; but your own fath-er said, "Give her up, don't both-er, the
how; soon you'll be cry-ing, on ac-count of all your ly-ing. Oh

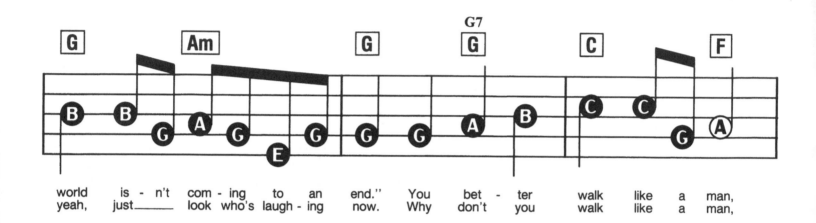

world is-n't com-ing to an end." You bet-ter walk like a man,
yeah, just____ look who's laugh-ing now. Why don't you walk like a man,

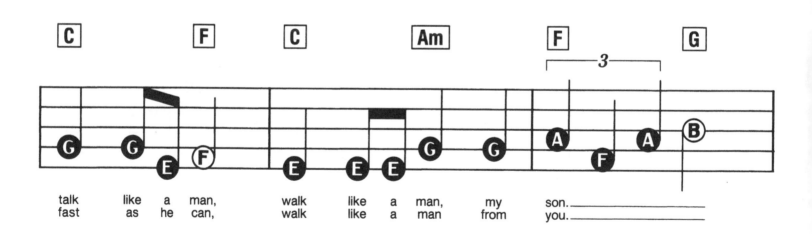

talk like a man, walk like a man, my son.____
fast as he can, walk like a man my from you.____

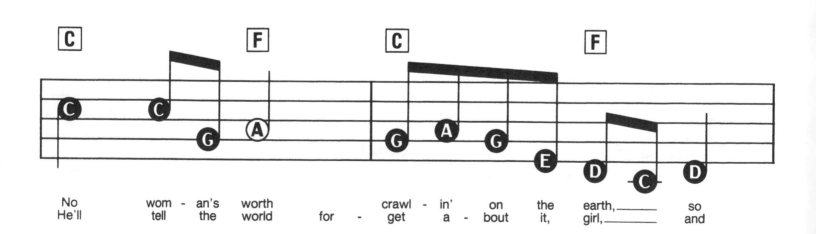

No wom-an's worth crawl-in' on the earth,____ so
He'll tell the world for-get a-bout it, girl,____ and

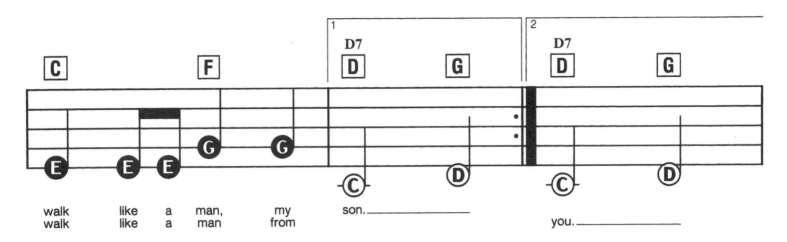

walk like a man, my son._____
walk like a man from you._____

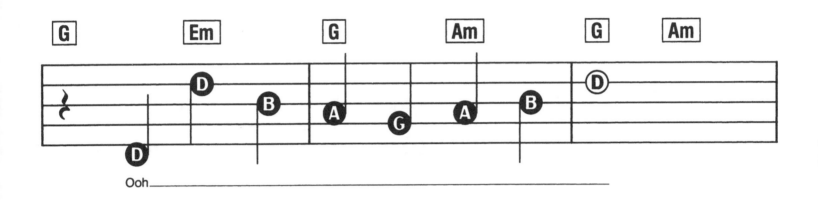

Ooh_____

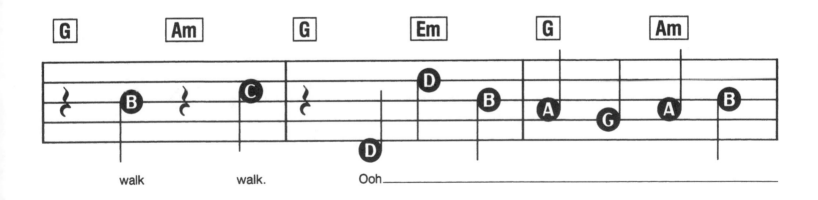

walk   walk.   Ooh_____

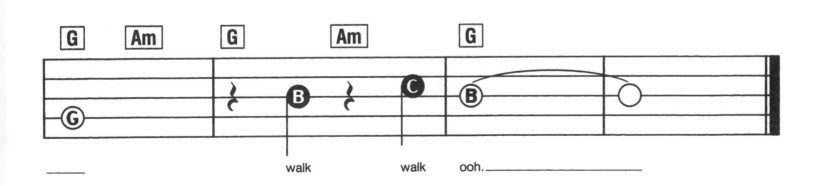

_____   walk   walk   ooh._____

Stay

Registration 2
Rhythm: Rock or 8-Beat

Words and Music by
Maurice Williams

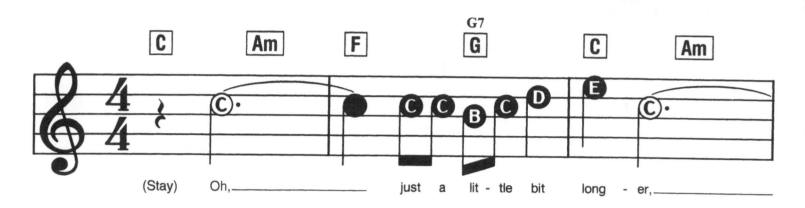

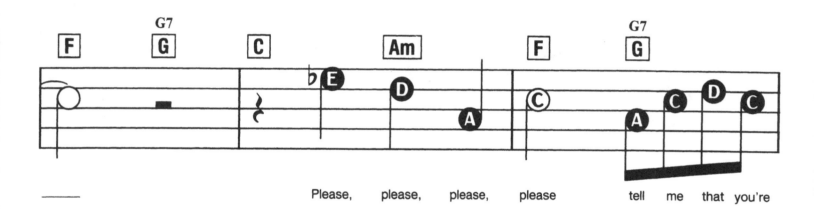

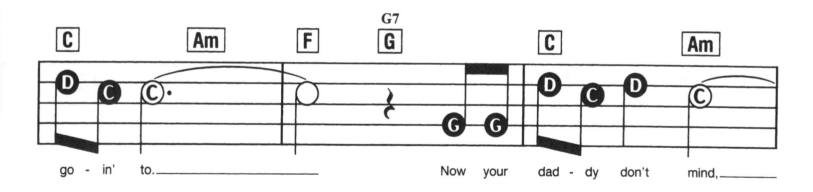

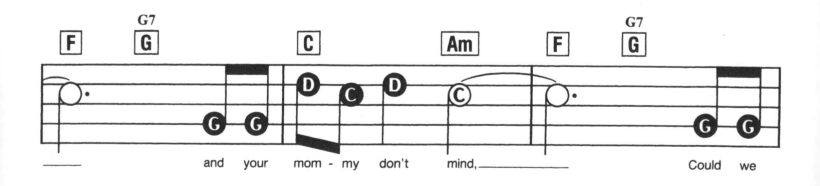

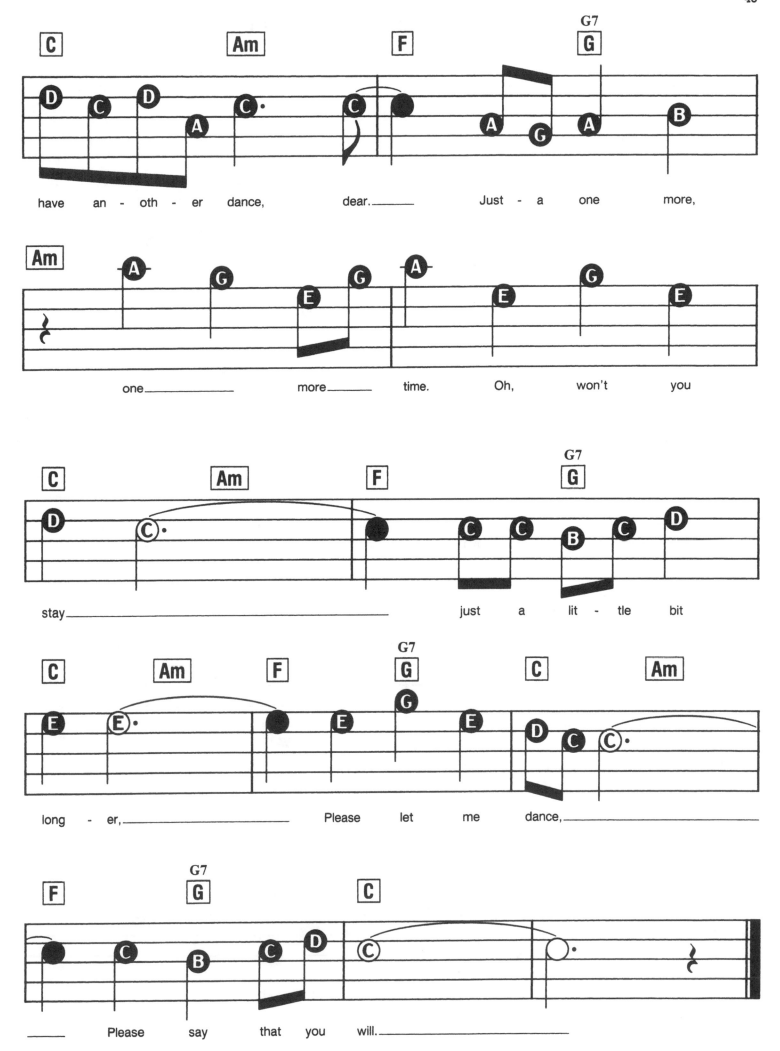

Who Loves You

Registration 7
Rhythm: Rock

Words and Music by Robert Gaudio
and Judy Parker

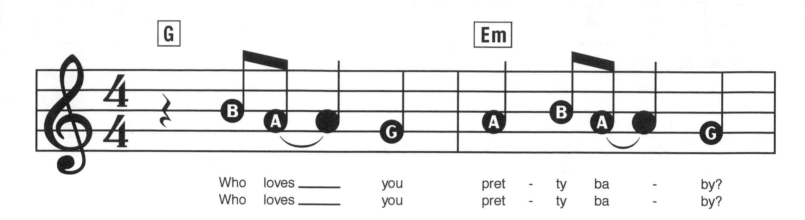

Who loves _____ you pret - ty ba - by?
Who loves _____ you pret - ty ba - by?

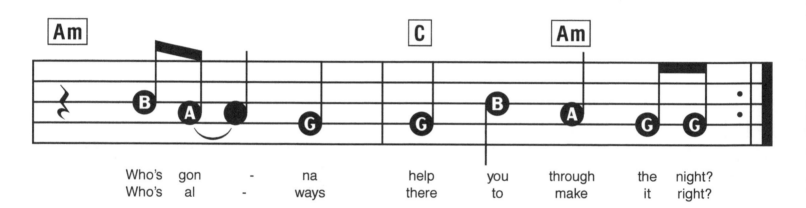

Who's gon - na help you through the night?
Who's al - ways there to make it right?

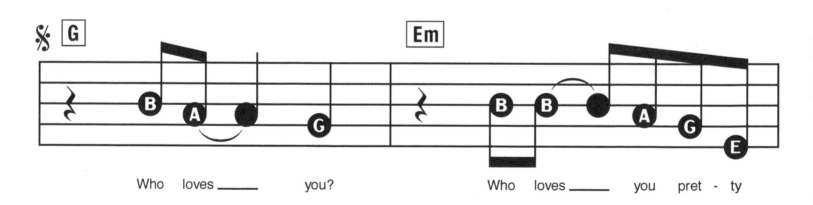

Who loves _____ you? Who loves _____ you pret - ty

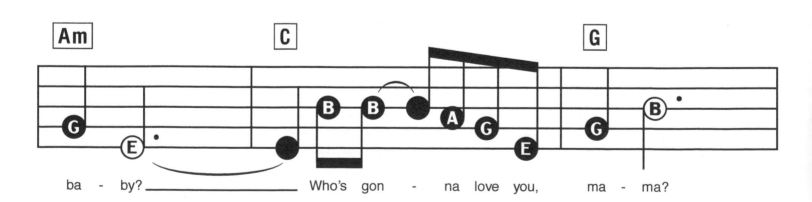

ba - by? _____ Who's gon - na love you, ma - ma?

47

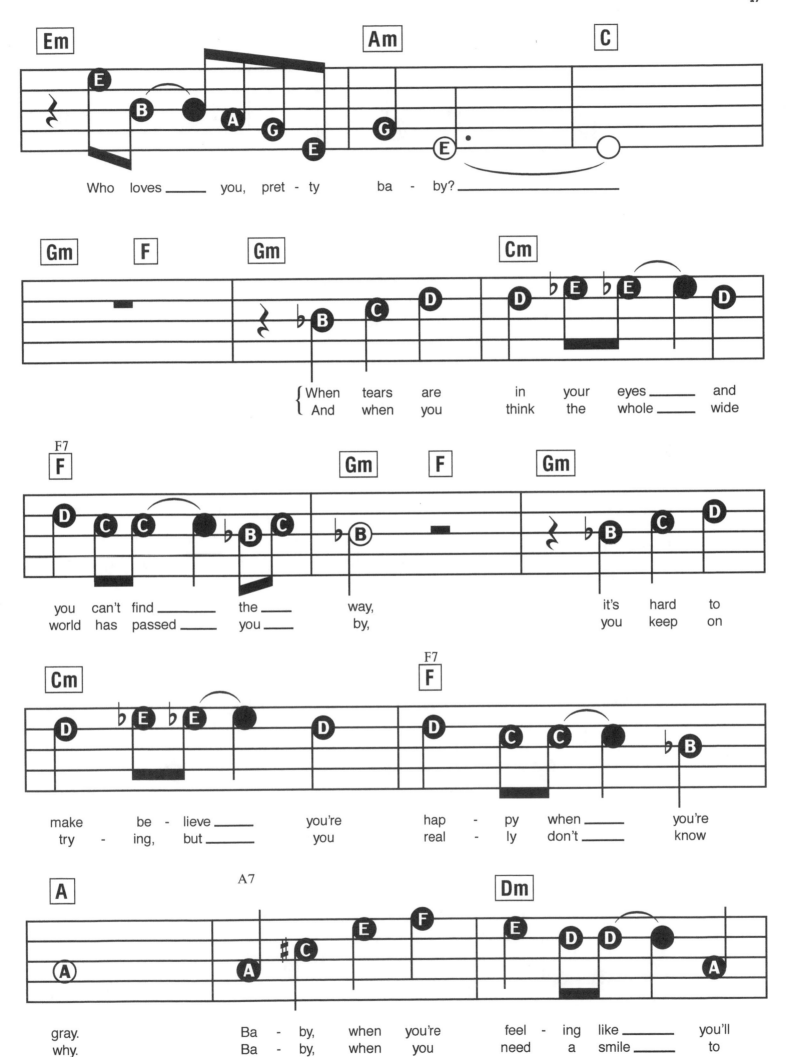

49

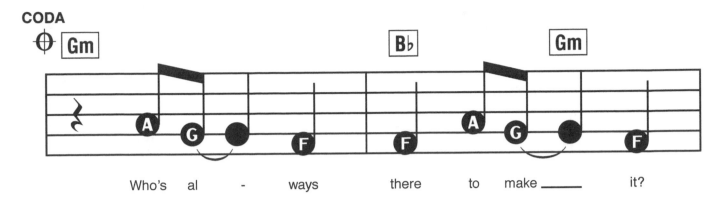

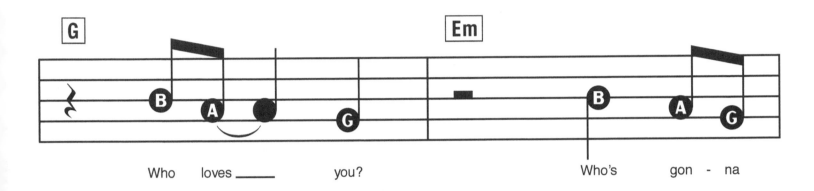

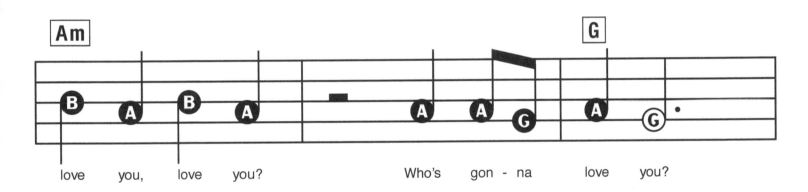

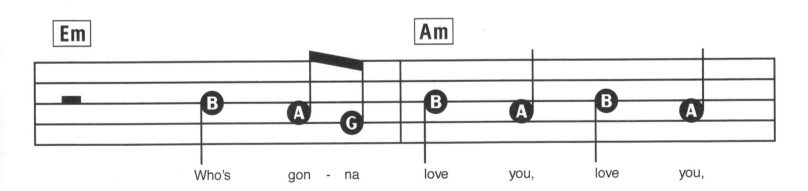

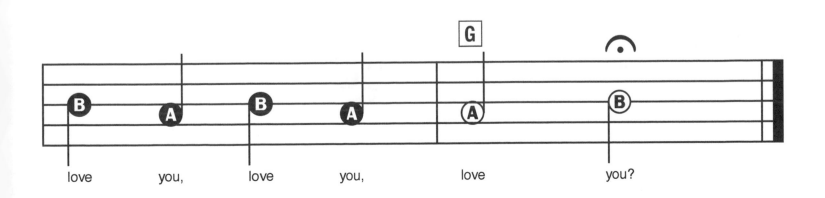

Working My Way Back to You

Registration 4
Rhythm: Rock or 8-Beat

Words and Music by Denny Randell
and Sandy Linzer

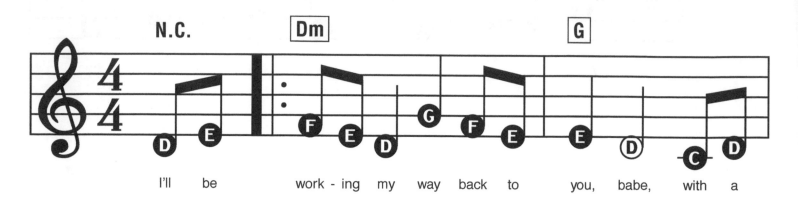

I'll be work - ing my way back to you, babe, with a

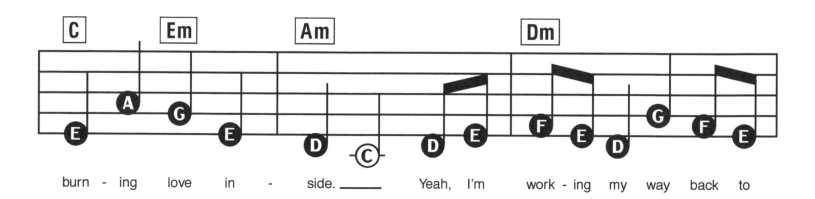

burn - ing love in - side. _____ Yeah, I'm work - ing my way back to

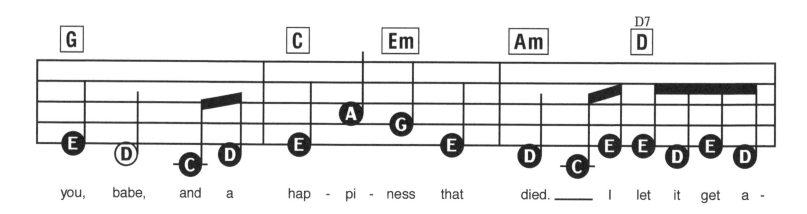

you, babe, and a hap - pi - ness that died. _____ I let it get a -

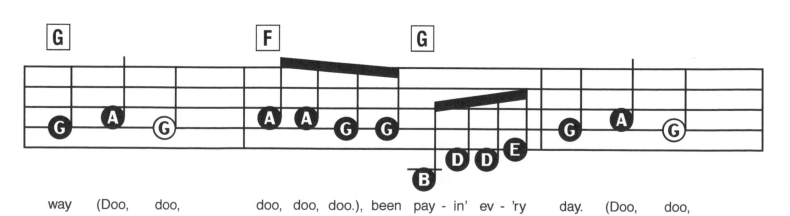

way (Doo, doo, doo, doo, doo.), been pay - in' ev - 'ry day. (Doo, doo,

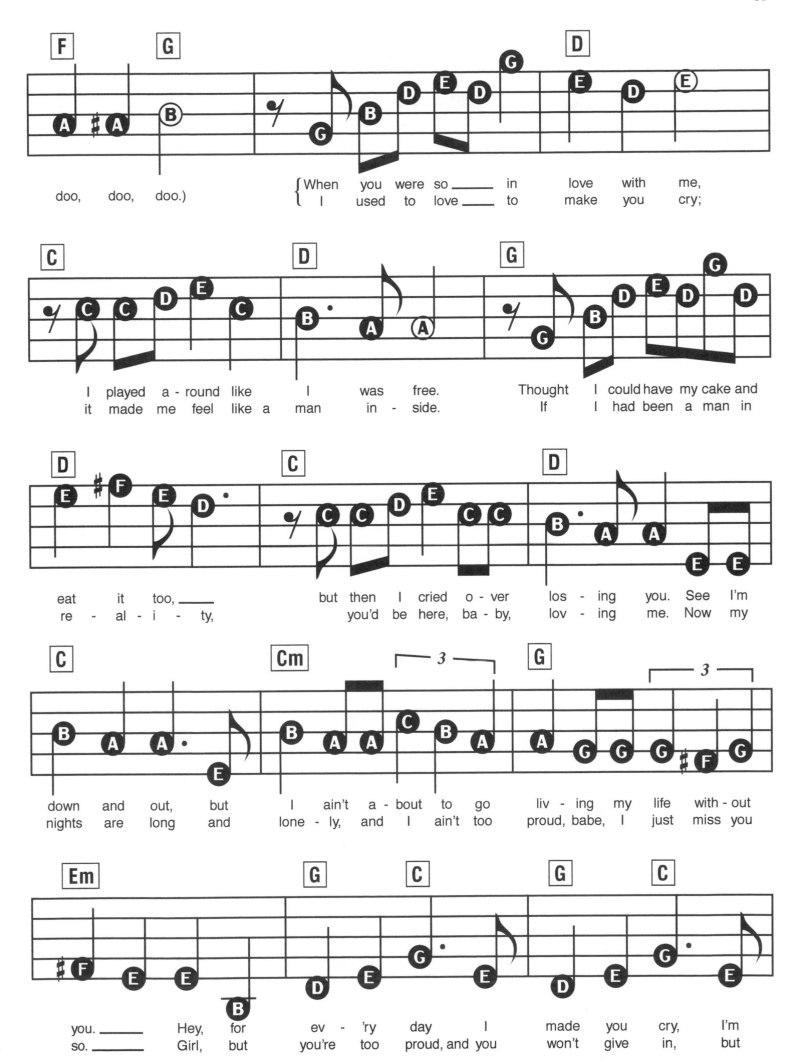

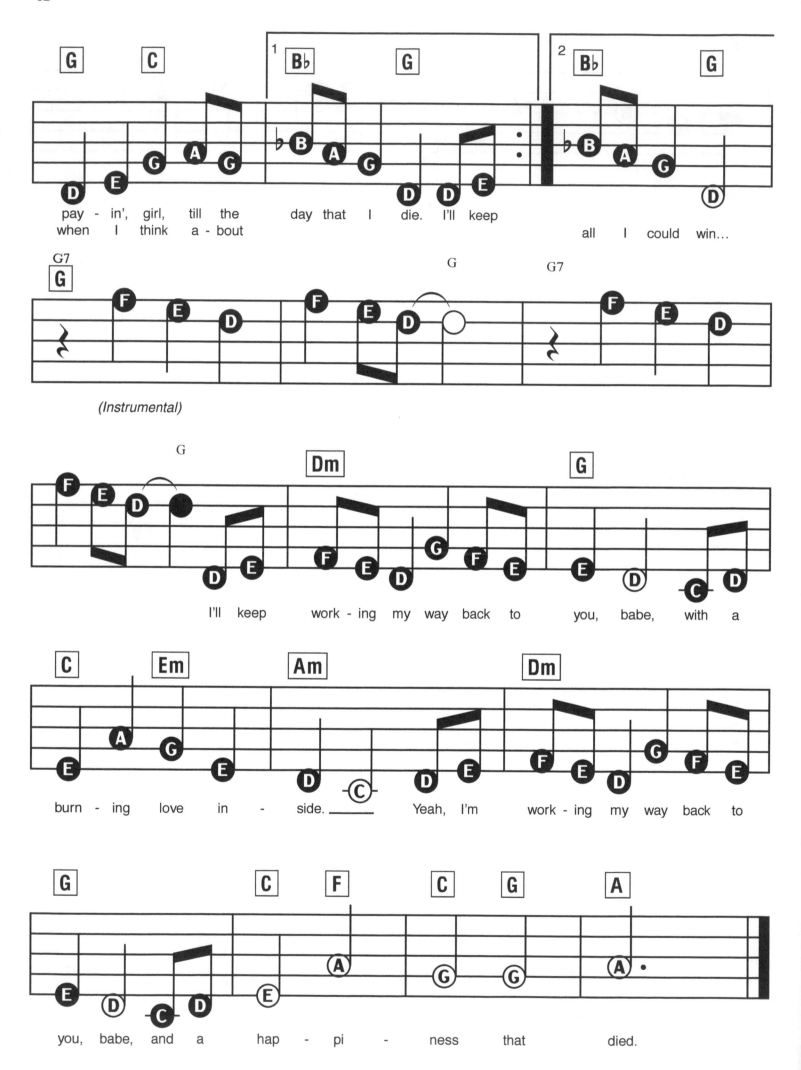

 # Registration Guide

- Match the Registration number on the song to the corresponding numbered category below. Select and activate an instrumental sound available on your instrument.

- Choose an automatic rhythm appropriate to the mood and style of the song. (Consult your Owner's Guide for proper operation of automatic rhythm features.)

- Adjust the tempo and volume controls to comfortable settings.

Registration

1	Mellow	Flutes, Clarinet, Oboe, Flugel Horn, Trombone, French Horn, Organ Flutes
2	Ensemble	Brass Section, Sax Section, Wind Ensemble, Full Organ, Theater Organ
3	Strings	Violin, Viola, Cello, Fiddle, String Ensemble, Pizzicato, Organ Strings
4	Guitars	Acoustic/Electric Guitars, Banjo, Mandolin, Dulcimer, Ukulele, Hawaiian Guitar
5	Mallets	Vibraphone, Marimba, Xylophone, Steel Drums, Bells, Celesta, Chimes
6	Liturgical	Pipe Organ, Hand Bells, Vocal Ensemble, Choir, Organ Flutes
7	Bright	Saxophones, Trumpet, Mute Trumpet, Synth Leads, Jazz/Gospel Organs
8	Piano	Piano, Electric Piano, Honky Tonk Piano, Harpsichord, Clavi
9	Novelty	Melodic Percussion, Wah Trumpet, Synth, Whistle, Kazoo, Perc. Organ
10	Bellows	Accordion, French Accordion, Mussette, Harmonica, Pump Organ, Bagpipes